"Sweet and Sassy"
Praying with Purpose

Belinda –

You have so much power to spread the message of God.

I pray ble ssing over you and your family –

MEREDITH BARRON *Sassy*

ISBN 978-1-0980-1363-9 (paperback)
ISBN 978-1-0980-1364-6 (digital)

Copyright © 2019 by Meredith Barron

All rights reserved. No part of this publication may be reproduced, distributed, or transmitted in any form or by any means, including photocopying, recording, or other electronic or mechanical methods without the prior written permission of the publisher. For permission requests, solicit the publisher via the address below.

Christian Faith Publishing, Inc.
832 Park Avenue
Meadville, PA 16335
www.christianfaithpublishing.com

Printed in the United States of America

January 1

Prayer for the Day

Father, here we stand facing a brand new year. We have no idea what it will hold or how it will turn out. For a lot of us, the old year brought grief and sorrow at the loss of a loved one or something so unexpected that we didn't know which way to turn. For others, there was joy because of new life, new opportunities. Everybody has their own memories of what the old year meant to them. I believe that we must accept God's will not only for each new year but for each new day. If we are still on this earth, we have things God wants us to accomplish. I don't understand the hows and whys of God's decisions, but I trust him enough to believe he makes no mistakes. Let us not give up our hope.

My prayer for today is that we embrace God's will in our life and remember that he gave all of us enough grace for every situation we are placed in.

Amen and thank you, Lord.

Thought for the Day

Fresh starts and new beginnings are ours for the taking.

January 2

Prayer for the Day

Father, I wonder how bad it hurts you when we shut you out of our life—no meditation or quiet time with you, no prayer time, no praise time. I know how much it bothers me when my child is upset or angry with me and doesn't speak to me because I have put my foot down or told him no. I think it is similar to how you feel knowing you created us to praise you and love you, yet so many times, we shut you out. I am certain that many times my life should have been taken, yet it wasn't. I can absolutely shout the victory, yet at times I remain silent and bottle up the hurts and disappointments. You are a true and living God who is able to supply all our needs according to your riches. Does it get any better than that?

My prayer for today is that we will always remember he did not ask us to be perfect to come to him. He simply asked us to come.

Amen and thank you, Lord.

Thought for the Day

Perfection is not a requirement to be loved by God.

January 3

Prayer for the Day

Father, I look in the mirror at my reflection sometimes, and I just want to break the mirror. I don't see myself the way you or even others see me. All I see is pain, mistakes, and messes. I don't know about you, but I am very hard on myself, very critical. Many of you may feel the same way, but if we remember that God doesn't look at us like that, we'll be satisfied with what we see. God sees a beautiful person that he handcrafted in the image of his likeness, so realizing that, he put us together exactly how he wanted us to be. We can smile and move on. We live in a world that judges on outward appearances. Let's look at others on the beauty of their heart, and the world will be a better place.

My prayer for today is that we will always have eyes that see the best in people no matter what they look like.

Amen and thank you, Lord.

Thought for the Day

What you see is what you get, but sometimes the best is something that can't be seen at all except through actions.

January 4

Prayer for the Day

Father, I love flowers. They are so beautiful to look at and bring so much enjoyment to the eye. They do require a little work, but it's worth it when the blooms burst forth, and you can enjoy them for their beauty. People are like flowers. Some need only a little tending to, and who knows what kind of beautiful blooms may burst forth? If flowers are not tended, they will wither and fade. Eventually, they will die. And so it is with people. All we need is a little tender, loving care to become a beautiful flower. Don't write people off just because they look a little faded or withered. We don't know what may be just waiting to bloom ever so beautifully.

My prayer for today is that we will take the time to tend to the people around us knowing there's something beautiful waiting to bloom and flourish.

Amen and thank you, Lord.

Thought for the Day

When you take time to tend to things, you end up with beautiful results.

January 5

Prayer for the Day

Father, the heart is such a small organ, but it is the very thing that keeps us alive. A heart can be full of joy, and then again it can be broken. Some say they guard their heart. Still others say they wear it on their sleeve. I have wondered about the condition of my own heart. Are pieces missing when I said I was heartbroken? Did it increase in size when it was filled with joy? Did it become defensive when I was guarding it or cold when I was wearing it on my sleeve? Never will I know the answers to these questions, but I am satisfied that God knows the condition of my heart. He specializes in these matters, and there's not a heart beating that he doesn't himself tend to.

My prayer for today is that we examine ourselves and be willing to let ourselves be guided by what we feel in our hearts.

Amen and thank you, Lord.

Thought for the Day

When you get to the heart of the matter, you'll get what matters to the heart.

January 6

Prayer for the Day

Father, we have had the sweetest couple doing some painting for us this week. They really have had some hard times lately, but they haven't let it affect their attitude. They're kind, grateful, and most of all, humble. I was strengthened by their willingness to not give up, yet if anybody had a reason to, it would have been them. I grumble about things that happen in my life because it seems easier to complain than to have hope and faith that things will get better. No, there are no instant cures, and if we have faith in our Father, he always makes a way when we didn't know the way. A fresh coat of paint put a fresh perspective on life for me.

My prayer for today is that we can trust God enough to know he hears our cries for help, and our struggle doesn't escape his watchful eye.

Amen and thank you, Lord.

Thought for the Day

Look at life with a fresh set of eyes and watch your focus change.

January 7

Prayer for the Day

Father, when we smile we see evidence of a smile because our face looks totally different. Also the same can be said for when there is no smile. Our faces are a mirror reaction to our feelings, and they are many different faces we show the world throughout the day. People react to what we show them from our faces. What will my face say about me?

My prayer for today is that we will always remember that any action will cause a reaction, and I pray we can just learn that there is always something to smile about.

Amen and thank you, Lord.

Thought for the Day

A smile looks good on you!
You should wear it more often.

January 8

Prayer for the Day

Father, distance can be measured with various instruments or tools, but if there is distance between you and a loved one, there is no way to tell how great the distance is, no way to measure the gap.

It feels like it just goes on forever, and you may think it will last forever. "Only time will tell" is a phrase we've all heard, but it's really the truth, and so we continue to pray for the gap of distance to close. I dislike conflict and strife and want to live at peace with everyone in the world even though I find myself conflicted or striving at times.

My prayer for today is that we will choose wisely our words and actions with everyone we come into contact with and remember that what breaks our heart touches yours.

Amen and thank you, Lord.

Thought for the Day

Instead of giving others a piece of your mind, try and have peace of mind.

January 9

Prayer for the Day

Father, we cannot remove bitterness on our own, and it will never be easy to accept that God wants to rescue even the people we dislike. We must allow God to change our heart as we work toward forgiving those who have hurt us. This will take time. God, we know that you ask that we be willing to let you begin to work in our hearts.

Amen and thank you, Lord.

Thought for the Day

When people have hurt us deeply, it is easy to hate them and want vengeance. Holding tightly to this bitterness and hatred can easily become a character defect.

January 10

Prayer for the Day

Father, some days I feel on top of the world, and on other days, I feel like the world is on top of me. I admire those among us who seem to always be in a good mood, a good frame of mind. It doesn't work that way for everyone else. When I feel like the world is on top of me, I remind myself that there will be a better day, a brighter tomorrow, and that no feeling is final. There is faith and hope as long as there is breath to be drawn. Try and think on things lovely and good, and in doing so, we may be able to hold on until our world is in balance again.

My prayer for today is that we never forget that we haven't made it this far by chance, and he who never sleeps nor slumbers won't put any more on us than we are able to handle.

Amen and thank you, Lord.

Thought for the Day

Tomorrow is a new day.

January 11

Prayer for the Day

Father, buildings and properties are restored every day. Lord, you specialize in the restoration of people. Oh, we can be run-down and may even look as if there is nothing to work with, but we are living proof that what looks like it should be condemned can be changed to something beautiful and better. Yes, there have to be changes made, and work has to take place; some things have to be done away with altogether, but the end result is magnificent. We came to you in a condemned condition and cried out for help. You did not fail us then, and you haven't failed us since. Our Father can't, won't live in a dwelling that is condemned, but he will live in a place that is willing to be restored.

My prayer for today is that we will always be willing to allow changes to be made by our Father so that we can be made beautiful by his restoration.

Amen and thank you, Lord.

Thought for the Day

We'll always be a work in progress. Make sure you're willing to give up what is not needed.

January 12

Prayer for the Day

Father, I prayed the same amount of time on my knees for my nephew as I did for my son, yet my nephew is in heaven with you, and my son is still here. My nephew left this world far too soon, yet you felt his work on earth was finished. I saw a strength from his mother that I didn't know she possessed. She had a quiet grace and dignity about her, yet I know she was in terrible agony. We all were. Death does that to people. It also makes us question our own mortality. We will never know the answers to these questions that death makes us ask ourselves, but you do. All I know for sure is I want to make each day count. I want to appreciate that I'm still here because you have work for me to do. I don't know what kind of work, but I'm sure it's very important.

My prayer for today is that we will consider carefully each day as a precious gift, and even if things look bad, you are good. You are so good.

Amen and thank you, Lord.

Thought for the Day

Why put off for tomorrow what can be done today?

January 13

Prayer for the Day

Father, why do we put so much pressure on ourselves? The word *pressure* even implies the use of force. I am always rushing here and there, and if I would just slow down, I would feel less pressured. Even my thoughts are racing and thinking of things I have to do next. There are twenty-four hours to each day. Isn't that enough?

My prayer for today is that we will take time to take care of ourselves and remember that you will take care of the rest.

Amen and thank you, Lord.

Thought for the Day

Put it in cruise control. You're still going to get where you're going. You will just be more relaxed when you get there.

January 14

Prayer for the Day

Father, I will try to keep my life calm and unruffled. This is my great task to find peace and acquire serenity. I must not harbor disturbing thoughts. No matter what fears, worries, and resentments I may have, I must try to think of constructive things until calmness returns. I pray that I may build up instead of tearing down. I pray that I may be constructive and not destructive.
Amen and thank you, Lord.

Thought for the Day

Only when I am calm can I act as a channel for God's spirit.

January 15

Prayer for the Day

Father, I believe that complete surrender of our lives to God is the foundation of serenity. God has prepared for us many mansions. Don't look upon that as referring only to the afterlife. Don't look upon this life as something to be struggled through in order to get the rewards of the next life. I pray that we may do God's will. I pray that such understanding, insight, and vision shall be ours now and shall make our life eternal here and now.

Amen and thank you, Lord.

Thought for the Day

I believe that the kingdom of God is within us, and we can enjoy eternal life here and now.

January 16

Prayer for the Day

Father, I know that the vision and power which I receive from you are limitless as far as spiritual things are concerned. In temporal and material things I must submit to limitations. I know that I cannot see the road ahead. I must go one step at a time because you do not grant me a longer view. I pray that in spite of my material limitations I may follow God's way. I pray that I may learn that trying to do your will is perfect freedom.

Amen and thank you, Lord.

Thought for the Day

I am in uncharted waters limited by my temporal and spatial life but unlimited in my spiritual life.

January 17

Prayer for the Day

I believe that God has all power. It is his will to give and his to withhold, but he will not withhold it from the person who dwells near him. It is breathed in by the person who lives in God's presence. I pray that I may get myself out of the way so that God's power may flow in. I pray that I may surrender myself to that power.
    Amen and thank you, Lord.

Thought for the Day

I will learn to live in God's presence, and then I will have those things which I desire of him—strength, power, and joy. God's power is available to all who need it and are willing to accept it.

January 18

Prayer for the Day

Father, I want to be one with the Divine Spirit of this universe. I will set my deepest affections on things spiritual, not on things material. As a man thinketh, so is he. So I will think of and desire that which will help and not hinder my spiritual growth. I pray that I may think love, and love will surround me. I pray that I may think health, and health will come to me.
    Amen and thank you, Lord.

Thought for the Day

No human aspiration can reach higher than this.

January 19

Prayer for the Day

Father, I will pray daily for faith, for it is God's gift. On faith alone depends the answer to my prayers. God gives it to me in response to my prayers because it is a necessary weapon for me to possess for the overcoming of all adverse conditions and the accomplishment of all good in my life. I pray that I may so think and live as to feed my faith in God. I pray that my faith may grow because with faith God's power becomes available to me.
    Amen and thank you, Lord.

Thought for the Day

Today, like the days that fell before, I will work on strengthening my faith.

January 20

Prayer for the Day

Father, it's so easy to leave our Bible closed and untouched, but the Bible is personal, a lamp for our path today and for the future. Reading the Bible offers guidance in any stage of life. It encourages us to forgive, to find hope, and to love well.

Dear God, thank you for the Bible and your guidance through it. I pray its words become an even brighter lamp for my path.

Thought for the Day

*As I seek guidance from my Bible today,
I will allow these principles of life to soak my soul.*

January 21

Prayer for the Day

Father, we know that following you in service is never easy, but it comes with a peaceful assurance. God will guide our steps and can cause good to come out of the worst situation. God brings order and peace out of the chaos of life's small pieces.

I pray, God of grace, to you, thanking you for your promise to deliver us from evil. May your love and mercy guide our actions so we may know peace each day.

Amen and thank you, Lord.

Thought for the Day

God wants me to have true peace.

January 22

Prayer for the Day

Father, often we are content only with the perfect, the unblemished, the new. That is not the way of God who understands that we are broken, imperfect, and damaged. At times we may feel ashamed at our brokenness, but in our suffering we are being made strong. That strength will develop character that clings to hope.

My prayer, Father, is to recognize that you give us enough strength to withstand the storms we encounter.

Thought for the Day

God transforms my suffering into strength.
PS. He's always on time no matter what I think.

January 23

Prayer for the Day

Father, I will learn to overcome myself because every blow to selfishness is used to shape the real, eternal, unperishable me. As I overcome myself, I gain that power which God releases in my soul, and I will be victorious. I pray, Father, that I may obey you and walk with you and listen to you. I pray that I may overcome my own selfishness.

Amen and thank you, Lord.

Thought for the Day

How can I do something new for God and my neighbor today?

January 24

Prayer for the Day

Father, every time I open my eyes to a new day, I am thankful. Each day, I strive to be a better person than I was the day before, even if I don't always succeed. There are many people who have faith in my new ways that I would never disappoint or let down because I may be that person they're measuring what they might achieve against. I do make mistakes. I will fail. It will not detour my path. My prayer for today is that some good thing will happen in a person's life who is struggling, and this good thing will renew their faith, and they will soar as eagles.

Amen and thank you, Lord.

Thought for the Day

Don't ever try to measure your value.
You are worth more than you can even imagine.

January 25

Prayer for the Day

Father, I will say thank you for everything, even the seeming trials and worries. I will strive to be grateful and humble. My whole attitude toward you will be one of gratitude. I will pass on what God reveals to me.

I pray that I may be grateful for the things I have received and did not deserve. I pray that this gratitude will make me truly humble. Amen and thank you, Lord.

Thought for the Day

I will be glad for these things I have received. I will pass on what God reveals to me. I believe that more truths will flow in me as I go along in life.

January 26

Prayer for the Day

Father, the Bible teaches us how to live by Jesus's example. He loved the poor, reached out to help the sick, and forgave those who hurt him. Still I ask myself, *Why is it so hard for me to live the same way?* Perhaps my soul becomes agitated by stress, by guilt over wrongs I have done, or by memories of times I have been hurt. When we find ourselves stumbling over such obstacles, we can allow God to calm these storms by singing songs of praise, praying for forgiveness, and focusing on our blessings. Father, I pray for the reviving of your Spirit in us so that we will reflect love to everyone around us.
    Amen and thank you, Lord.

Thought for the Day

Focusing on our blessings causes the inner disturbances to subside; then we become more able to reflect the beauty and light of God's love.

January 27

Prayer for the Day

Father, I came to you in faith, and I know you gave me a new way of life. This new way of life has altered my whole existence, the words I speak, the influence I have. They will spring from the life within me.

I pray that I may learn the principles of the good life and not forget them when things get tough. I pray that I may meditate upon them and work at them because they are eternal.

Amen and thank you, Lord.

Thought for the Day

I see how important is the work of a person who has this new way of life. The words and the example of such a person can have a wide influence for good in the world.

January 28

Prayer for the Day

Father, I will have faith no matter what may befall me. I will be patient even in the midst of troubles. I will not fear the strain of life because I believe that you know just what I can bear. I will look to the future with confidence.

I pray I may put this day in the hands of you, God. I pray for faith so that nothing will upset me or weaken my determination to detour me from this journey I'm on.

Amen and thank you, Lord.

Thought for the Day

I know that God will not ask me to bear anything that could overcome or destroy me.

January 29

Prayer for the Day

Father, I know that my life will not be immune from difficulties, but I will have peace even in difficulties. I know that serenity is the result of faithful, trusting acceptance of God's will even in the midst of difficulties. I pray that I may welcome difficulties. I pray that they may test my strength and build my character.

Amen and thank you, Lord.

Thought for the Day

Saint Paul said, "Our light afflictions, which are but for a moment, work for us a far more exceeding and eternal weight of glory."

January 30

Prayer for the Day

Father, in silence comes your meaning to the heart. I cannot judge when it enters the heart. I can only judge by the results. God's word is spoken to the secret places of my heart, and in some hour of temptation, I find that word and realize its value for the first time. When I need it, I find it there.

I pray that I may see your meaning in my life. I pray I may gladly accept what you have to teach me.

Amen and thank you, Lord.

Thought for the Day

"Thy Father, who seeth in secret, shall reward thee openly."

January 31

Prayer for the Day

Father, today is a new day that will never happen again. On this day, everything is new. Today there will be new insights from God, new encounters, new opportunities for me to share the love of Christ, new service opportunities, and new blessings. Father, I pray that my ear is always turned to hear your voice.

Amen and thank you, Lord.

Thought for the Day

Each day God offers us the opportunity to renew our relationships with our neighbors. Each day brings something new and gives us the chance to experience and share God's love in new ways.

February 1

Prayer for the Day

Heavenly Father, thank you, Lord, for a day called *today*. Amen and thank you, Lord.

Thought for the Day

Today is a gift. Unwrap it carefully.

February 2

Prayer for the Day

Heavenly Father, thank you for another day. Even though I hate getting wet, thank you for the rain, for all the good gifts you give your children.
Amen and thank you, Lord.

Thought for the Day

Another day, I'm all in.

February 3

Prayer for the Day

Heavenly Father, another day has come and how thankful we are. I pray, Father, that our hearts remain pure and untouched by the ugliness that surrounds us and instead focus on those things that are pure and lovely.

Praying for one heart to soften today, one mind-set to change. Amen and thank you, Lord.

Thought for the Day

Life is full of twists and turns, but the Father is the captain of this ship.

February 4

Prayer for the Day

Heavenly Father, another day has come for me thank you, Lord. My prayer is to be satisfied with knowing your timing is always perfect. The veil has been lifted, and the blood was loosed so many years ago, but that same blood then is still the same blood today. How comforting. Renew my mind and heart today; Lord, I pray.

Amen and thank you, Lord.

Thought for the Day

As I journey with Jesus, I never have to worry about being late. He, for sure, is an on-time God.

February 5

Prayer for the Day

Heavenly Father, thank you, Lord, for the opening of my eyes. My body is healthy, and my mind is sound. Thank you. I've never had to walk the path of life alone.

You left the Comforter here to hold my hand. I am not fearful or scared of things as I once was. I am enveloped with peace and very contented with my life. Thank you; when I pray, you're right there listening and making good decisions about my lot in life.

Amen and thank you, Lord.

Thought for the Day

Look out world! Here comes the child of a King!

February 6

Prayer for the Day

Heavenly Father, thank you that you know the utterances of our hearts. Amen and thank you, Lord.

Thought for the Day

Farther along we'll understand why.

February 7

Prayer for the Day

Heavenly Father, thank you for the sunshine in my face and the breeze on my back. I am so thankful for this contentment in my soul, the happiness in my heart. I pray, dear Lord, to always remember and never forget that you are the trusted One. I will praise you and love you while I am *here* and rejoice in knowing that I will be able to praise you and love you when I get *there*. I pray God's people will turn to you and not from you. Bless the ones that read this prayer, Lord, according to your riches and thy will.

Amen and thank you, Lord.

Thought for the Day

The anchor holds.

February 8

Prayer for the Day

Father, I will start a new life each day. I will put the old mistakes away and start anew each day. God always offers us a fresh start. I will not be burdened or anxious. If God's forgiveness were only for the righteous and those who had not sinned, where would be its need? I pray that my life may not be spoiled by worry and fear and selfishness. I pray that I may have a glad, thankful, and humble heart.

Amen and thank you, Lord.

Thought for the Day

I believe that God forgives us all of our sins if we are honestly trying to live today the way he wants us to live. God forgives us much, and we should be very grateful.

February 9

Prayer for the Day

I will practice love because lack of love will block the way. I will try to see good in all people, those I like and those who fret me and go against the grain. They are all God's children, and I will try to give love; otherwise, how can I dwell in God's spirit whence nothing unloving can come? I pray that I may do all I can to love others in spite of their (my) faults, and I pray that as I love, so will I be loved.

Amen and thank you, Lord.

Thought for the Day

I will try to get along with all people because the more love I give away, the more I will have.

February 10

Prayer for the Day

Father, I believe that my faith and God's power can accomplish anything in human relationships. There is no limit to what these two things can do in this field. Only believe and anything can happen. I pray that I may strengthen my faith day by day. I pray that I will rely more and more on God's power, leaning not on my own understanding.

Amen and thank you, Lord.

Thought for the Day

All walls that divide us from other human beings can fall by our faith and God's power. These are the two essentials. Everyone can be moved by these.

February 11

Prayer for the Day

Father, I know that you cannot teach anyone who is trusting in a crutch. Let us throw away all our crutches and walk in your power and spirit. God's power will so invigorate us that we shall indeed walk to victory. I pray that we may have more and more dependence on you, Lord. I pray we throw away all our crutches and let your power take its place.

Amen and thank you, Lord.

Thought for the Day

There is no limit to God's power.
Let us go step by step, one day at a time.
God's will shall be revealed to us as we go forward.

February 12

Prayer for the Day

Father, I believe that life is a school in which I must learn spiritual things. I must trust you and let you teach me. I must listen to you and let you speak to my mind. I must commune with you in spite of all opposition and every obstacle. I pray that I may regularly go to school in things of the spirit. I pray that I may grow spiritually by making a practice of these things.

Amen and thank you, Lord.

Thought for the Day

If I make a life habit of schooling myself in spiritual things, God will reveal himself to me in so many ways.

February 13

Prayer for the Day

Father, I know you find amidst the crowd a few people who follow you just to be near you, just to dwell in your presence. A longing in the eternal heart may be satisfied by these few people. I will let God know that I seek him just to dwell in his presence to be near him, not so much for teaching or a message as just for him.

I pray that I may have a listening ear so that God may speak to me. I pray that I may have a waiting heart so that God may come to me.

Amen and thank you, Lord.

Thought for the Day

It may be the longing of the human heart to be loved for itself; it is something caught from the great divine heart.

February 14

Prayer for the Day

Father, I know your love is totally different from ours. Your love is not based on a feeling but flows from your very nature. In contrast, human love can fluctuate or fail in times of disagreements or conflict. I pray that I will not let any circumstance dictate how I respond or react, and I will walk it out, walk in love.

Amen and thank you, Lord.

Thought for the Day

God's love is perfect and eternal. We did not build it, so we cannot dismantle it. He places no conditions on his love, none whatsoever.

February 15

Prayer for the Day

Father, I know I must rely on you. I must trust you to the limit. I must depend on your divine power in all my relationships. I will wait and trust and hope until you show me the way. I will wait for guidance in each important decision. I will meet the test of waiting until a thing seems right before I do it. I pray that I may not go off on my own.
  Amen and thank you, Lord.

Thought for the Day

*Every work for God must meet the test of time.
The guidance will come if I wait for it.*

February 16

Prayer for the Day

Father, the lifeline, the line of rescue, is the line from the soul to God. On one end of the lifeline is our faith, and on the other end is God's power. It can be a strong line, and no soul can be overwhelmed who is linked to God by it. I will trust this lifeline and never be afraid. I pray that no lack of trust or fearfulness will make me disloyal to God. I pray that I may keep a strong hold on the lifeline of faith.

Amen and thank you, Lord.

Thought for the Day

God will save me from doing wrong and the cares and troubles of life. I will look to God for help and trust him for aid when I am emotionally upset.

February 17

Prayer for the Day

Father, I believe you have already seen my heart's needs before I cried to you and before I was conscious of these needs myself. I believe you have already prepared the answer. God, I know you do not have to be petitioned with sighs and tears and much speaking before you lose the desired help. I pray that I may understand my real wants and needs. I pray that my understanding of these needs and wants may help to bring the answer to them.

Amen and thank you, Lord.

Thought for the Day

God has already anticipated my every want and need. I will try to see this as his plans unfold in my life.

February 19

Prayer for the Day

Father, as we fight the good fight of faith today, let us remember this that our mind is where the battle will take place. When thoughts come that are contrary to God's will, cast them down. Worry is meditating the thoughts of Satan. You are guaranteed victory because God has promised us triumph in Christ. If we don't buy into Satan's lies, they cannot come to pass in our life.

Amen and thank you, Lord.

Thought for the Day

When you recognize that you are worrying, stop it immediately. Replace worried, fearful, and doubtless thoughts with the Word!

February 20

Prayer for the Day

Father, we know it is when the goal is in sight that heart and nerves and muscles and courage are strained almost to the breaking point. It is so with us. The goal of the spiritual life is in sight. All we need is the final effort. The saddest records are made by people who ran well with brace and stout hearts until the sight of the goal, and then some weakness or self-indulgence held them back. They never knew how near the goal they were or how near they were to victory. I pray that we may press on until the goal is reached. I pray that we not give up in the final stretch.

 Amen and thank you, Lord.

Thought for the Day

Don't ever—I mean ever—give up.

February 21

Prayer for the Day

Father, I know I must keep a time apart with you every day. Gradually I will be transformed mentally and spiritually. It is not the praying so much as just being in your presence. The strengthening and curative powers of this I cannot understand because such knowledge is beyond human understanding, but I can experience them. The poor, sick world would be cured if every day each soul waited before God for the inspiration to live aright. I pray that I may faithfully keep a quiet time apart with you, Lord. I pray that I may grow spiritually each day.

Amen and thank you, Lord.

Thought for the Day

Our greatest spiritual growth occurs in our time spent with God.

February 22

Prayer for the Day

Father, the world doesn't need supermen or superwomen, do we? We need supernatural people, people who will turn the self out of their lives and let the divine power work through them. Let inspiration take the place of aspiration. Seek to grow spiritually rather than to acquire fame and riches. Our chief ambition should be to be used by God. The divine force is sufficient for all the spiritual work in the world. I pray that we can be an instrument of the divine power. I pray that I may do my share in remaking the world.

Amen and thank you, Lord.

Thought for the Day

God's instruments, we, his beloved children, can remake the world.

February 23

Prayer for the Day

Father, I will try to be unruffled no matter what happens. I will keep my emotions in check, although others about me are letting theirs go. I will keep calm in the face of disturbance, keep that deep, inner calm through all the experiences of the day. In the rush of work and worry, the deep, inner silence is necessary to keep me on an even keel. I pray that I may be still and commune with you. I pray that I may learn patience, humility, and peace.

Amen and thank you, Lord.

Thought for the Day

I must learn to take the calm with me into the most hurried days, especially the hurried days.

February 24

Prayer for the Day

Father, I count my blessings daily, and I know I am who I am because of who you are in me. I surely count it as a blessing when someone I love and respect asks something of me. It is not that it makes me feel important but that I am to be counted on, trustworthy to them. Father, I pray that you'll continue to allow me to do my best to let my light shine.

Amen and thank you, Lord.

Thought for the Day

Don't count me out; count me all in! Praying blessings and peace to your world today. You make it a better one by being in it. Love you, guys.

February 25

Prayer for the Day

Father, we live in a world that hurts us every day. It gets confusing and at the least frustrating as we navigate the course of life. There is always pain, too much I think, but my thoughts are not his thoughts, so I have to remember that he knows where we are and what we're going through. I pray, God, for the grace to be strong as these next days are upon us.

Amen and thank you, Lord.

Thought for the Day

I can't and won't rely on my own strength. It's not sufficient, but his will carry me through.

February 26

Prayer for the Day

Father, life is taken for granted, especially when you are young. Only as we grow older do we realize how quickly it can all change in the blink of an eye. I am thankful for my faith and the love of the ones who care about me when I'm hurting. I know there is a purpose for every bit of your plan, and even though I don't understand, I must trust that one day your purpose will be revealed. For all who took time to read and respond to my repeated yet grief-stricken posts and pictures, I pray you will bless them, Lord, for their hearts are filled with love and compassion.

Thought for the Day

Love is the glue that holds the children of God together.

February 27

Prayer for the Day

Father, I am convinced that all you do has a purpose. I will take the trials of life and walk like a winner knowing I am privy to a great plan even if I don't understand what that plan is. You know, and that's good enough for me. Help me, Lord, each day to grow and flourish, producing a good harvest of fruit.

Amen and thank you, Lord.

Thought for the Day

Don't look back. Don't look ahead; just look around. There's plenty to work with.

February 28

Prayer for the Day

Father, each day is a celebration to worship you and recognize you as the Lord and Master of our lives. We lack for nothing when we walk hand in hand with you. These last days have not been easy for our family, but we choose to focus on those things that are lovely and good and not on things that will tear us apart or cause us grief and sorrow. My prayer is to make my mark in my lifetime to help others along life's way. May God bless you with your heart's desires and always remember and never forget that we are all the apple of God's eye.

Amen and thank you, Lord.

Thought for the Day

We can't all hit the high notes, but we can all sing in harmony for our precious Lord.

March 1

Prayer for the Day

Father, we know you care about all of our challenges, even the seemingly trivial ones. Our Creator wants to be involved in every part of our lives. When we remember that God is bigger than our worries and concerns, we can approach God with a thankful heart. Lord, I pray that we will bring all our concerns to you no matter how small.

Amen and thank you, Lord.

Thought for the Day

The broken road led me to my desired destination.

March 2

Prayer for the Day

Father, you have called us to have a childlike faith, and children have many questions, and so it is with us. We may question God, but we never need to doubt him. Things that are a mystery to us now will be revealed one day, and so live in the now trusting that God knows who you are, where you are, and what you need. I pray that my faith will continue to grow daily but especially when I am faced with the darkness of the valley.

Amen and thank you, Lord.

Thought for the Day

This world is the home we know; eternity is the home that awaits us.

March 3

Prayer for the Day

Father, we are your foot soldiers on this earth, working on the behalf of our loved ones that right now are not capable of fighting the war for themselves. We, warriors, are not fighting in the natural but in the supernatural, pulling down strongholds and claiming victory since we know we have the mightiest warrior of all on our side—you.

I pray, Father, we never give up. We may grow weary, but we will not give up until the fight is over.

Amen and thank you, Lord.

Thought for the Day

Be prepared to do battle every day. Satan never rests. Personally I say, "Go back to hell, devil. Your lies and tricks won't work with God's people."

March 4

Prayer for the Day

Father, it's been a hard year for me and my family with hardships and disappointments, but we made it through and have grown from these things. We know that we are children of a God that loves us unconditionally. Nothing we do can make him love us more or less. As I look back, I celebrate life, and all I have experienced knowing God has been with me through it all. I pray, Lord, to count the hard times as a time of faith and growth and continue to praise you and have faith that your way is not only the best way. It's the only way.

Amen and thank you, Lord.

Thought for the Day

I'm standing on the blood, remembering those outstretched arms of his on the cross.

March 5

Prayer for the Day

Father, I don't care how tough times get. I will never turn my back on you again. You're my strength, my only hope, and in you I place my trust.
Amen and thank you, Lord.

Thought for the Day

*He will draw you as close
as you'll allow him to.*

March 6

Prayer for the Day

Father, thank you for the sunshine. I thank you for your grace and mercy that has sustained me, Lord; for those standing on the mountaintop, let them shout the victory. For those that are in the valley, may they remember it's only temporary. I pray, Lord, that we all realize you are able and willing to give us our hearts' desires. Amen and thank you, Lord.

Thought for the Day

Peace of mind can't be bought but is priceless.

March 7

Prayer for the Day

Father, getting up early has so many advantages! The birds are singing, and it's the perfect time for reflection on all the beauty you created for our enjoyment. I'm thankful for another day here, and I will do my best, be my best, and give you my best. Thank you for seeing in me what I could not see in myself. I pray, Lord, that all your children come to the realization that without you, we're nothing, but with you, we're a force to be reckoned with!

Thought for the Day

It's a beautiful morning. I think I'll go out and shine.

March 8

Prayer for the Day

Father, there is nothing more precious than family, spending time with the ones you love laughing, talking, just being together. For families that are holding grudges, forgive and move on. We are not promised a tomorrow. I pray that we hold our loved ones close and do our best to love our neighbor, walking in peace and harmony.

Amen and thank you, Lord.

Thought for the Day

Family—the ones that God gave us handpicked.

March 9

Prayer for the Day

Father, another day has come for us, and this is not promised. Let us make the most of each day you give us, rejoicing always in the knowledge that we, the children of God, are your foot soldiers doing the work on earth that must be accomplished. I pray, Lord, that none should perish; each person present themselves to you for refining that is needful to all. Life can be complicated, yet we make it more complicated than it has to be. I pray, Father, that for those who are undecided about their salvation can make that solid decision to place all hope in you.

Amen and thank you, Lord.

Thought for the Day

With the Lord on your side you can't lose.

March 10

Prayer for the Day

Father, I have prayed a long time about a certain situation and had others praying with me. Never think God isn't listening or working things out for the best. I am starting to see the fruits of our prayers. He really is an on-time God. My prayer today is this: Don't ever give up or let Satan trick you into giving up.

Amen and thank you, Lord.

Thought for the Day

Every day is a new beginning, a chance again; give it your best shot!

March 11

Prayer for the Day

Father, I know we are just passing through, and this is not our home, but while we are here, let us do all we can to make this world a better place. The sunshine gives my heart hope for some good things to happen today, and I know that if we run into trouble, we just have to call your name. I'm thankful that I have hope eternal. I sleep well at night because of this knowledge.

I pray that if anyone is being tried by the fire that you know that it will not last, and you will be stronger than you were before.

Amen and thank you, Lord.

Thought for the Day

There is joy in the journey.

March 12

Prayer for the Day

The years really roll by, and you look up, and you're wondering, "What have I done? Have I left my mark, made an impression on anyone's life? How much good seed have I sown?" I want to make a difference in someone's life, a lot of people's lives while on earth. My prayer for today is that if you know me or read my posts, if you need me, I'll be there. That is my prayer, Lord. Let people know I am here to guide or help them in any way I can.

Amen and thank you, Lord.

Thought for the Day

There is one that sticketh closer than a brother.

March 13

Prayer for the Day

Father, thank you for another day! Life is good, and I'm thankful to be alive. I want to always be listening to hear from you instead of rushing to and from. I will make mistakes, and instead of letting them weigh me down, I will consider it to be a teachable moment. God's children are the salt of the earth, and we must use the flavor of our salt to help others who struggle. God, I want always to use the talents you have gifted me with to make this world a better place.

Amen and thank you, Lord.

Thought for the Day

We all have so much to offer. Never let anyone make you feel like you have no value. Oh, you are so precious in his sight.

March 14

Prayer for the Day

Father, as we awaken this morning with the breeze blowing, we know that the sun will follow. No day is the same as the day that was called yesterday. Let us put on the mind-set of Christ and the full armor of God and focus on being the very best we can be. Your Word tells us you will never leave us or forsake us, so we must not worry about things that only you have control over. That gives me good reason to pull myself up by my bootstraps and give the Lord a shout for the victory that has already been won!

Amen and thank you, Lord.

Thought for the Day

Life is not always a smooth ride, but if you're buckled up beside the Master, he'll help you hang on!

March 15

Prayer for the Day

Father, one day after a while, every knee shall bow, and every tongue confess that Jesus is Lord. I pray for my family, loved ones, and friends that none shall perish. I know that all days aren't *perfect*, for I am a living witness that even soldiers get weary, but I know what to do when I do grow weary. My prayer for everyone today is that if you've grown weary, gain strength from his Word. He cannot lie, and he said he would never leave nor forsake us.

Amen and thank you, Lord.

Thought for the Day

Heads up! If you fail, God always allows you an opportunity to retest, so now you know! Love ya!

March 16

Prayer for the Day

Father, thank you for goodness and mercy. At the end of the day, I pray to always have been the person you wanted me to be. I know I don't always succeed, and you know before I do where I may fail or falter. My heart loves your people, and I am thankful I have so much love placed in my heart by you. I pray, Lord, to never let life deceive me nor Satan trick me. I know you will never let anything pluck me from your hand.

Amen and thank you, Lord.

Thought for the Day

The sheep know the shepherds voice.

March 17

Prayer for the Day

Father, it's easy to take things for granted. I feel like it's supposed to be that way. Reality is, all we have comes from you, even the hard times. I shout when I'm standing on the mountain, but I've learned to shout while in the valley. I know so many that have rough patches in life, including me, but I am going to hang on to you with all my might and praise your holy name through it all. Lord, I pray to touch a life today, inspire someone with my enthusiasm about you.

Amen and thank you, Lord.

Thought for the Day

You're not ten feet tall and bulletproof, but we serve a God that is and so much more.

March 18

Prayer for the Day

Father, I have learned to accept people as they are even if I wish they were different because my duty is to love them, not to judge them. We will go through many trials while on this earth and face many hurts, but if we cling to you, the one that will stick closer than a brother, all will be well. I pray, Lord, that I can give myself to you completely, withholding nothing so that you can use me in any manner you see fit.

Amen and thank you, Lord.

Thought for the Day

Submission is not the same as giving up.

March 19

Prayer for the Day

Father, another day has been given. Don't take that lightly; none are promised. No matter the struggle, having a relationship with Jesus is assurance that you have been heard. He will bring you out of bondage. He will make a way where once there wasn't. He will dust you off and set you back on your feet. Ask me how I know these things. Surely most of you know my story, and if so, then you already know. If you don't, ask me. I know.

I pray to always be a willing vessel that others might want to *know*. Amen and thank you, Lord.

Thought for the Day

The best thing I have ever done was to truly grasp what I have in my salvation.

March 20

Prayer for the Day

Father, a new week is ahead of us. How we choose to live it is up to us. I'm choosing to grumble less and count my blessings more. There are so many needing our prayers. If you want to be used in the kingdom of God, there is something right at your doorstep. We all struggle in life. How we overcome the struggle depends on where you place your trust. I place my hope in Jesus Christ, and though I may fail at times, he doesn't keep score. My prayer is that before I depend on my own strength, on his I will depend first.

Thought for the Day

We are the foot soldiers on the ground for the kingdom. Be prepared to do battle everywhere you go.

March 21

Prayer for the Day

Father, I know I am a blessed woman. I look back on my life and know that you had plans that I knew nothing about. I have an irrefutable testimony to your mercy and grace that I am prepared to share anywhere, everywhere I go. My prayer today, Lord, that we will celebrate our salvation and know that you are still on the throne no matter what life throws at us.

Amen and thank you, Lord.

Thought for the Day

In a world where you can be anything you want, just be yourself.

March 22

Prayer for the Day

Father, we do live in a world where evildoing is on the increase, and it will continue until the day you bring us home. Until that time comes, we shall not live in fear or be fearful of anything but shall remain faithful to our Father who will always sustain us. My prayer is that we never forget and always remember he knows where we are, and he will never leave us nor forsake us.

Amen and thank you, Lord.

Thought for the Day

Have a beautiful day, and do a good deed and keep it a secret.

March 23

Prayer for the Day

Father, let us not look back, for that is done. Let us not look ahead, for only you know what is before us. Let us live in the now, for this is where we are. Father, I pray to have listening ears and a willing heart.

Amen and thank you, Lord.

Thought for the Day

Live in today. It's plenty.

March 24

Prayer for the Day

Father, I have seen time and time again that no matter the circumstances, you will be glorified. We get panicked and confused, and then after the panic and confusion have subsided, we step back and know you were there from the beginning. My prayer is that I never let that slippery serpent get any glory. My praise belongs to the King, not a king but the King.
Amen and thank you, Lord.

Thought for the Day

If our Father takes care to see the lilies so beautifully dressed, what do you think he will do for his children?

March 25

Prayer for the Day

Father, I am thankful that we're never too big to dream. You instilled something in us that makes us to want to be better and do better. Material things are worth nothing unless you enjoy a life that is based on a Christian lifestyle. We're going to make mistakes, but I won't let a mistake keep me down. I'm going to learn from it and move forward.

Amen and thank you, Lord.

Thought for the Day

We are gifted with our own set of talents. God will never call you to do something he won't equip you for.

March 26

Prayer for the Day

Father, we will face many things on earth that hurt us or even give us a moment or two of despair, but a true woman of God may falter, but she will never fail.

Listen now, all times won't and can't be smooth, but don't you ever give up on God. He never gave up on you.

Amen and thank you, Lord.

Thought for the Day

On my knees I learned to stand.

March 27

Prayer for the Day

Father, we lift our voices to praise you! I'm so thankful for another day to worship the King. Even in my darkest hour, you are there. You're worthy of all I have because you gave all you had. Amen and thank you, Lord.

Thought for the Day

Yes, it's Monday, but we're here, and that means hope is still at hand. Love ya! Blessings on your day!

March 28

Prayer for the Day

Father, so many battles are won or lost in our own mind. Satan will take an inch and run with it, so I know that I must stay on my guard, or I'll be defeated before I even get going good. I pray that when I feel myself slipping, even a little, I can remember that power of him in me and never forget that the battle has already been won.

Amen and thank you, Lord.

Thought for the Day

I think I can. I think I can. I know I can!

March 29

Prayer for the Day

Father, no day is like the one that fell before it or may fall after it. Our needs change, and that's okay. We know you are a God that does not change like the shifting sand. How comforting to know that no matter where we are in life, there you are. I pray, Lord, to always remember and never forget that I am the apple of your eye.
    Amen and thank you, Lord.

Thought for the Day

Since the apple doesn't fall far from the tree, I am my Father's child!

March 30

Prayer for the Day

Father, let us live in peace knowing that you have us in your hand, and nothing or no one can pluck us from it.
Amen and thank you, Lord.

Thought for the Day

It's a great day to be alive!

March 31

Prayer for the Day

Father, as long as I live, I will place my hope in you. I pray that the ones who are weak will turn to you for strength and for those that have strength to be fortified to be even stronger. Amen and thank you, Lord.

Thought for the Day

May you live in that place of peacefulness.

April 1

Prayer for the Day

Heavenly Father, another day has called our name, so we must live it to the fullest. It could be our last. We don't know. What we do know is that you will be beside us every minute. How comforting that is.

Amen and thank you, Lord.

Thought for the Day

As far as the east is to the west, all the opportunities in between are limitless.

April 2

Prayer for the Day

Heavenly Father, you woke me up this morning. What a blessing that you have given me another opportunity; what I do with it is up to me. I know life is but a few days of struggle, and then we will be with you in glory and struggle for nothing. If I struggle, let it be to be a better person each day.

Amen and thank you, Lord.

Thought for the Day

Since there is power in the blood, there is power in our blood as his blood runs through us.

April 3

Prayer for the Day

Heavenly Father, again today my plate is full, so much to do and take care of. Mentally, I can't comprehend, but physically, I just have to put one foot in front of the other. Able am I because of you. Whew. Thank you. I'm tired, but I'm strong through your strength that guides me.

Amen and thank you, Lord.

Thought for the Day

Father, you put a song in my heart and a pep to my step.

April 4

Prayer for the Day

Heavenly Father, thank you, Lord, for a willing spirit that lives within me telling me, "You can do anything you set your mind to." Always with me you are.

I pray to be in your perfect will today, and when I'm not, I know you'll chastise me and correct me.

Amen and thank you, Lord.

Thought for the Day

He corrects those he loves.

April 5

Prayer for the Day

Heavenly Father, here another day has come. Thank you. I feel your loving presence, and I embrace your strength. On my own and left on my own, I will mess things up. With you as my guide, I know my prayers are heard, and the blessings are distributed.

Amen and thank you, Lord.

Thought for the Day

Your portion is waiting.

April 6

Prayer for the Day

Heavenly Father, here we are waking up to another day. Some didn't make it to see another day. I'm thankful I did. Let me be exactly who I need to be today to be pleasing unto your sight. I have learned that each day brings its own set of challenges, but when I ask for help, I'll be sure and receive it. My heart cries out for you, and I pray, Lord, for one mind, one heart to be changed today.

Amen and thank you, Lord.

Thought for the Day

If you don't step up and take a swing, you'll never know if you can hit a ball out of the park.

April 7

Prayer for the Day

Heavenly Father, I guess the passing of time makes things easier. I pray it does. I don't know when reality will actually hit, but I know you'll be there to pick me up. Just when I think things are going all right, something happens, and I'm back to that place of feeling helpless again through your strength.
    Amen and thank you, Lord.

Thought for the Day

Just when I think I've got all my ducks in a row, one of them waddles off.

April 8

Prayer for the Day

Heavenly Father, thank you for another day. Blessed I was to wake up. How I proceed is up to me, but no matter, I'll be needing your help. I pray, God, to be a good person, the kind of person that is pleasing unto your sight, helping people and praying to make their lives better because they asked me and depended on me to do it.

Amen and thank you, Lord.

Thought for the Day

You are precious. Allow the Lord to take your hand.

April 9

Prayer for the Day

Heavenly Father, it's hard to live without regrets. You think of so many things you shouldn't have done or think you should have done. Reality tells you. You did all you could; it was just time. I know my sorrow is natural, Lord, but I pray to process my emotions in a way that brings peace to my soul.

Amen and thank you, Lord.

Thought for the Day

I'll only miss you until I'm finished with my work on earth. Then I shall join you in his eternal home.

April 10

Prayer for the Day

Heavenly Father, good morning! I'm awake and ready to tackle another day of life. You did this! You created me to be a person full of spunk and spirit, so bring it on life! Lord, I pray to always honor you in my thoughts and actions.

Amen and thank you, Lord.

Thought for the Day

Bah, humbug? Not today, Satan. Poof! You're gone.

April 11

Prayer for the Day

Heavenly Father, I'm thankful, God, for another day on this earth. I do worry about what will happen when I get older and then old; who will take care of me physically? I am grateful for the opportunity I had to spend time with my loved one and help her as her days grew shorter. We didn't know she would be gone so soon. I keep telling myself we did all we could. I guess that's how everybody feels when they lose someone they love. I pray, Lord, to make my time on this earth count.

Amen and thank you, Lord.

Thought for the Day

I've sat in your chair. I've slept in your bed. I've worn your bathrobe every morning because I wanted to feel you. I want you to know I'll do my best. Let's all pull together for a better world.

April 12

Prayer for the Day

Heavenly Father, I lift my family up to you in prayer. Some live close by; others don't. Still you know where they are. A son to keep safe, stress to be eased, a grandchild to be seen more often, mind-sets to change—the list goes on. I pray there is a lifting of burdens and joy in their hearts.

Amen and thank you, Lord.

Thought for the Day

If you shake the family nut tree, a few will always fall out. Love 'em anyway.

April 13

Prayer for the Day

Heavenly Father, the wind howls and blows around me, but I am safe. I pray for the safety of others. Throughout life, the storms will come, but I pray to always be forever in the favor of God, and my house will stand. Praying, Lord, today we will be pleasing unto your sight.

Amen and thank you, Lord.

Thought for the Day

My foot is on the rock, and my name is on the roll. Bring it!

April 14

Prayer for the Day

Heavenly Father, thank you for all things that we call life. The valleys become mountains, and we stand there shouting the victory. All times won't be easy, but we know they are manageable because of your spirit that cheers us on.

Amen and thank you, Lord.

Thought for the Day

Everybody can't do everything, but everybody can do something. Be somebody's something today.

April 15

Prayer for the Day

Heavenly Father, I sit here in peace looking at the flowers, watching the birds at the feeder. Everything is quiet and peaceful. In a little while, everybody will be waking up, yet I can hold onto to my peace because of your presence, and for that, I'm thankful. I pray, Lord, for a washing of my soul from the ugliness we are at times surrounded with.

Amen and thank you, Lord.

Thought for the Day

A peaceful, easy feeling will never let you down.

April 16

Prayer for the Day

Heavenly Father, so much has changed, and so much is different. I pray, Lord, that I can only grow from life's experiences. Growth at times is painful, I must say, but faith holds your hand to lead, guide, and direct.

Amen and thank you, Lord.

Thought for the Day

If we walk by faith and not by sight, we must look ahead and up, not down and back.

April 17

Prayer for the Day

Heavenly Father, thank you, God. Today is a brand-new day, and no feeling is final. I feel stronger today, and as always, I will be needing you to steer my ship.
Amen and thank you, Lord.

Thought for the Day

My ship may take on a little water, but it will never sink.

April 18

Prayer for the Day

Heavenly Father, today is a big day for us, and we need you to know we trust you. I pray, Lord, that we will not be afraid because you left the Comforter to hold our hand. We pray, Lord, to see the best in others and always have a willing spirit.

Amen and thank you, Lord.

Thought for the Day

Although the chaos is around me, I will remember that small still voice that is always my guide.

April 19

Prayer for the Day

Heavenly Father, thank you for another day on this earth and being clean. I pray, Lord, for those that survived addiction to keep fighting and those that are still fighting to win their battle. Lord, I know you are still on the throne. I see too many miracles everyday not to believe.

Amen and thank you, Lord.

Thought for the Day

When you get discouraged and downtrodden, like water off a duck's back, lemme hear you go, "Quack, quack." Get back in line, my little duck.

April 20

Prayer for the Day

Heavenly Father, good morning, and thank you I'm able to walk across the floor. Some can't. I pray, Lord, for those who are hanging by a thread with decisions that could change their entire life. Each day is so different from the one before and the one that will follow yet. They're all the same in one aspect. You are there to lead, guide, and direct.

Amen and thank you, Lord.

Thought for the Day

Slow and steady wins the race.

April 21

Prayer for the Day

Heavenly Father, thank you for another day. I have accomplished so much throughout my life, but my greatest accomplishment was the day I gave my heart and life to you. From that day forward, I knew I wasn't traveling this road of life alone. All days are doable as long as I stand on your promises because you cannot lie. When I pray, if I ask amiss, forgive me, Lord, as I know you always know best.

Amen and thank you, Lord.

Thought for the Day

Your credit card may be maxed out, but you'll never max out God's goodness. As long as we're breathing, the possibilities are endless.

April 22

Prayer for the Day

Heavenly Father, I pray for more patience. I've been a little aggravated and stressed lately, and I don't like me that way. Amen and thank you, Lord.

Thought for the Day

Try your servant Job. Now that's the kind of faith I want to have. When the devil whispers in your ear, you shout back, "I belong to the Lord."

April 23

Prayer for the Day

Heavenly Father, thank you that Christians around the world have a reason to celebrate daily but especially today. Amen and thank you, Lord.

Thought for the Day

This is it. Make no mistake. He is risen!

April 24

Prayer for the Day

Heavenly Father, praying today will be like yesterday filled with the knowledge that you rose yesterday to conquer every day.
Amen and thank you, Lord.

Thought for the Day

Let the celebration of a risen Savior continue.

April 25

Prayer for the Day

Heavenly Father, I pray to have eyes to always see the best in people. Amen and thank you, Lord.

Thought for the Day

The Lord said, "Forgive your neighbor seventy times seven times daily." Do the math. (All day, every day.)

April 26

Prayer for the Day

Heavenly Father, thank you for another day on earth. I have a burden I've been carrying around for a long time, and I know my prayer will be answered, so I'm in the *waiting room* to see your work.

Amen and thank you, Lord.

Thought for the Day

I'm not perfect. I'm just trying to be better.

April 27

Prayer for the Day

Heavenly Father, thank you, Lord, for the sun that comes after the rain. It's like the storms of life. They don't stay forever, but they rumble loud while they're here. We will make it in this life, and glory land comes after! That's something to shout about!

Amen and thank you, Lord.

Thought for the Day

Keep the faith always. He knows where you are. I haven't told you lately, my friends, that I love you so. I love you!

April 28

Prayer for the Day

Heavenly Father, I praise your holy name, and I am thankful that you've given me another day on earth, another chance to be better than I was yesterday. I pray, Lord, to never forget and to always remember that you and you alone are the beginning and the end. I am yours, and I am the apple of your eye.

Amen and thank you, Lord.

Thought for the Day

Be all you can be. God gifted you with special talents, and using our talents brings glory to his name.

April 29

Prayer for the Day

Heavenly Father, thank you for being a God that loves unconditionally. I pray, Lord, to show the same unconditional love to others. I pray, Lord, to not expect anything from any man, relying on and solely being dependent upon you. Amen and thank you, Lord.

Thought for the Day

Who you ask depends on what you get. Ask the One that was able to create this world with a thought. That's the One that can make it happen.

April 30

Prayer for the Day

Heavenly Father, I hear the birds tweeting back and forth. They have no worries, so why should I? It speaks plain about this in your Word. I pray, Lord, to not *over-respond* to remain calm. I pray that I can slow down and realize everything doesn't have to happen right then! Ahh, let your Spirit be my guide.
    Amen and thank you, Lord.

Thought for the Day

In a world that changes day by day, minute by minute, it's comforting to know he is the same yesterday, today, and always. Whew, just a little note to self.

May 1

Prayer for the Day

Father, somewhere someone had plans for today that didn't make it through the night. Somebody somewhere won't make it through today. My prayer is that in their last moment they felt your loving arms around them.

Amen and thank you, Lord.

Thought for the Day

Man makes many plans. God is the ultimate event planner. In him I place my hope.

May 2

Prayer for the Day

Father, the wind blows, and there you are. The birds sing, and there you are. When I stumble and need you, there you are. You are my ever-present help in time of need. I may not stumble as much this week as I did last week, but no matter when I stumble or how hard I stumble, there you are.

Amen and thank you, Lord.

Thought for the Day

If nothing ever changes, nothing will ever change.
It's not about turn or burn, but it is about him.

May 3

Prayer for the Day

Father, I have had many ups and downs in my life, but one thing that remained constant was I knew there was a God, and I knew he loved me. My conversion began in a jail cell, but it was real, not jailhouse religion. That was my darkest hour, and in my darkest hour, he sent the Comforter to hold my hand and soothe my broken heart. Today in my darkest hours, the Comforter is with me, and I know I am never alone. I pray, Lord, I have pleased you.

Amen and thank you, Lord.

Thought for the Day

You may feel all alone in this world, but there is One who never sleeps nor slumbers. He keeps watch all night; his shift never ends.

May 4

Prayer for the Day

Father, I know faithfulness does not ensure a life without storms or shipwrecks, yet I know you guarantee that your presence and power will be with us when we arrive at our ultimate destination. When the storms of life rage around me, Lord, let me call for you and never forget that you, Lord, are the Master of the wind.

Amen and thank you, Lord.

Thought for the Day

We are assured by faith of a positive outcome, but it is usually attained by persevering through difficult times.

May 5

Prayer for the Day

Father, I give thanks always for the work you have done in me. I still sin, but through forgiveness, I move on. No sins are less or more than others. All sins are equal, but none are unforgivable. I pray for everyone to feel the power that the Holy Spirit gives them and how I pray we all use this power to help others transform their lives.

Amen and thank you, Lord.

Thought for the Day

In Jesus, we have the power.

May 6

Prayer for the Day

Father, I am not ashamed of my past, although I do wish I hadn't been so determined to do things my way. Thank you, God, for never leaving me nor giving up on me. You saw in me things I couldn't see when I looked in the mirror. As I look in the mirror today, I am satisfied that when I say, "Thy will be done," I'll receive the very best you have to offer.

Amen and thank you, Lord.

Thought for the Day

Are you satisfied that in your heart you're giving God the best and not the rest?

May 7

Prayer for the Day

Father, thank you for the gift of life and change. I once prayed mightily for others I loved to change. God, I see how that was not good, so I began to pray for the change to begin within me. As I grow stronger in my walk with you, I change, and because of my changing, I see others in a more loving light, and so I see that it was I that needed to change. You are good, Lord, to show me these things. Amen and thank you, Lord.

Thought for the Day

It is not my place to take my brother's or sister's inventory. My place is to love them and help them daily. Everyone needs our love and support.

May 8

Prayer for the Day

Father, I know you deliberately choose things that the world considers foolish in order to shame those who think they are wise, and you choose those who are powerless to shame those who are powerful. I pray, Lord, to never question, "Why me?" when I stumble along the way. "Why not me?" will be my answer, for I have seen my share of evil, and I know that goodness and mercy will win every time.

Amen and thank you, Lord.

Thought for the Day

We all stumble. How you pick up and recover is up to you.

May 9

Prayer for the Day

Father, thank you for your word. I praise you, for you are holy and merciful. Lord, I pray to decrease so that I may see you increase. I have journeyed a long way, yet the journey begins anew each day.

Amen and thank you, Lord.

Thought for the Day

Weeping may endure for the night, but joy will come in the morning. It isn't ever over unless you quit. P.S. If no one has told you they love you lately, I love you. Praying your day is blessed with joy untold.

May 10

Prayer for the Day

Father, thank you for a feeling of peacefulness that surpasses all understanding. I know in my heart that I am able because you are faithful. I pray that I never let fear hold me back. Amen and thank you, Lord.

Thought for the Day

Since we know that what is bound on earth is bound in heaven, claim your vision and operate with the knowledge of God's power.

May 11

Prayer for the Day

Father, we have another day to be thankful for! All we have is a gift and not to be taken lightly. Today I am praying for wisdom and discernment of the truth. I know I have much power given to me by the Holy Spirit, so instead of worrying about my *problems*, I will pray and speak to the mountains that I face. I may even shout to the mountains I face. They are not unmovable.

Amen and thank you, Lord.

Thought for the Day

Today is a good day to take control of the things that trouble your heart.

May 12

Prayer for the Day

Father, the greatest gift I've ever received was my salvation. It cost me nothing and you everything. I am close with all of my family and each one so precious to me. Thank you for a loving church family that are family by your blood. I may fail, Lord, but I will never quit. I pray, God, to be about your business, setting all other business to the side, and being a foot solider for the kingdom of Christ is my mission.

Amen and thank you, Lord.

Thought for the Day

We all are called by God.
It is our decision on how we answer.

May 13

Prayer for the Day

Father, thank you for the very breath in my body. I am so thankful for all you have done for me and grateful that you're not finished with me. I will always be a work in progress. I pray, Lord, to be willing to accept what I cannot change and live with the knowledge that I don't have control, yet I know the One that does.
   Amen and thank you, Lord.

Thought for the Day

If we were perfect, there would be no need for grace.

May 14

Prayer for the Day

Father, today is a new day and a chance to be better than I was yesterday! My heart wants to hold as much love for man as yours did to live, love, and forgive. Always, Lord, use me. I'm willing and able because you see what I never did. Praise God; here I come!

    Amen and thank you, Lord.

Thought for the Day

He's a good, good Father.

May 15

Prayer for the Day

Father, I feel so blessed to be your child. You are never far from my heart, and I am comforted by your nearness when I feel alone. In an ever-changing world, I can hold on to the one thing that remains constant—Jesus Christ. In you I place my hope. Amen and thank you, Lord.

Thought for the Day

The Lord says that I am valuable, capable, and usable. I'm going to take him at his word.

May 16

Prayer for the Day

Father, there are times when our inner well runs dry. We need periods of solitude to replenish, to connect with you and our inner self to quiet our minds. I do believe we are here on earth to connect with people, to help one another, remembering the importance of staying connected.

My prayer is that you strengthen me to be a light for you.

Thought for the Day

We are the light. Don't ever think you don't or can't shine.

May 17

Prayer for the Day

Father, good morning to all God's children and the sunshine! Little things do mean a lot, so take time to enjoy the gifts God has given. I pray, Lord, for all the prayer requests I've seen or heard and pray thy will be done.
Amen and thank you, Lord.

Thought for the Day

It's really all up to each person how they choose to change their own little part of the world we live in.

May 18

Prayer for the Day

Father, help me to listen when you are speaking. Amen and thank you, Lord.

Thought for the Day

There are two voices you should always listen to. One is the voice of God; the other is the voice of experience.

May 19

Prayer for the Day

Father, so many things can shake our confidence and knock us off course. If we stay grounded in the knowledge that you are our ever-present help, all will be well.

Thought for the Day

When we allow our emotions to rule over what God says, we position ourselves for failure.

May 20

Prayer for the Day

Father, to *let go and let God* is a simple set of words but have much meaning. Why do I feel like I have to worry when I have the privilege of coming before you with my petitions? My prayer for today is to truly grasp the meaning of faith.
　　Amen and thank you, Lord.

Thought for the Day

We never have to worry that our needs go unnoticed. He never sleeps nor slumbers.

May 21

Prayer for the Day

Father, we know if we are believers, we are commissioned to make disciples for you. No one is too hopeless, too far, or too dirty for God's reach. My prayer is that none should perish but remember that David was a man after God's own heart, and he sinned but was a repentant man. May we all be willing to ask for forgiveness.

Amen and thank you, Lord.

Thought for the Day

We all have a testimony that someone needs to hear.

May 22

Prayer for the Day

Father, I will always remember the cross. I pray that I will have a good influence on someone's life today.
   Amen and thank you, Lord.

Thought for the Day

Just hang on to what you know is truth.

May 23

Prayer for the Day

Father, I am going to do great things with my life. My prayer, Lord, is to always remember to ask you what direction I should go.
Amen and thank you, Lord.

Thought for the Day

When God is in it, little is much.

May 24

Prayer for the Day

Father, if being uncomfortable or in a tough situation causes me to learn and grow, I'm all for it. The voice of experience will always be a winner, and I am always going to be a winner because God loves me, and he doesn't keep score concerning my mistakes. That is something to smile about, Lord. Lord, my prayer is to never stop growing and to be a better person than I was yesterday.
    Amen and thank you, Lord.

Thought for the Day

The world is a wide-open adventure.
Where is it taking you?

May 25

Prayer for the Day

Father, only you can bring comfort to our broken hearts. We don't utilize the gifts you have given us. We have power in our bodies to do so much, yet we let it lie stale and dormant. I pray that all believers will start pulling down the strongholds of addiction in our community. It's going to take all of us, but change will come if we exercise our faith.

Amen and thank you, Lord.

Thought for the Day

Faith is like a muscle. You must exercise it daily.

May 26

Prayer for the Day

Father, I'm the kind of person that wants everyone to enjoy a good life. I want everyone to have a *good ride*, but no matter what I want, the other people I want good things for have to put forth some effort too. My prayer for today is that a great understanding will come to those that are struggling. Lord, touch them in their spirit so that we all can live in that place called *normal*.

Amen and thank you, Lord.

Thought for the Day

The struggle is real, but don't struggle against the help that can and will save you.

May 27

Prayer for the Day

Father, today seems like an ordinary day, but the truth is I'm going to be very busy doing your work. I have a fire in me that I'm going to do all I can for as many as I can to let them feel the love you so purposely placed in us. My prayer for today is that all God's children find the willingness to serve you.

Amen and thank you, Lord.

Thought for the Day

Find your passion, and you'll find your purpose.

May 28

Prayer for the Day

Father, when I moved out of the way to allow you to do your work, the relief was instant. I know that what you put together, no man can undo. My prayer for today is to not worry and believe that you are not slow to act but instead know *it* will come out perfect.

Amen and thank you, Lord.

Thought for the Day

In childlike trust, that's when faith begins.

May 29

Prayer for the Day

Father, sometimes I make life harder than it is intended to be because of me trying to fix everything and everyone. You, the Master, knows all and sees all. My prayer for the day is to continue to trust you in all situations. You know what is breaking my heart, and I know you are working on this situation for us.

Amen and thank you, Lord.

Thought for the Day

His eyes are on the sparrow as he watches over me.

May 30

Prayer for the Day

Father, another day has come for us. It was not promised. My prayer for today is that we do not take life lightly, yet we do not take ourselves too seriously.
Amen and thank you, Lord.

Thought for the Day

The truly grateful and humble person who is always praising God is not tempted to do wrong.

May 31

Prayer for the Day

Father, good glorious morning to all! I am walking in love today and feeling good about all things since I laid my burdens down.
I am encouraged when I spend time with your people, realizing everyone has something or someone that causes them to really put forth an effort when they pray. My prayer for today is to not be discouraged but encouraged knowing the victory has already been won!
Amen and thank you, Lord.

Thought for the Day

Sing as if you are singing to the Lord himself.

June 1

Prayer for the Day

Father, I am praying about several situations right now. Regarding these, I have been praying a long time. I have no doubt that my prayers have been heard in heaven, and I do not doubt even for a moment that you are working these prayers out for the best. I may never understand your ways or your timing, but I do know for sure that what God puts in place, no man, nothing can put asunder. Until these prayers are worked out by you, Lord, may peace live in the hearts of those who are waiting for an answer. May God's grace always be enough for them and me.

Amen and thank you, Lord.

Thought for the Day

Realizing that his timing is always perfect makes sitting in the waiting room more bearable.

June 2

Prayer for the Day

Father, I reflect daily on how far I have come, yet I'll never finish my work here until you come for me or call us home. Daily I grow stronger as I read your Word, studying to show thyself approved. Life is not perfect, and it never will be, yet I don't dwell on these things. I dwell on what I have been taught concerning these things. I have learned to praise you always and be ready at a moment's notice to share my testimony. Someone needs to hear what I have experienced to share my hope to give others hope.

Amen and thank you, Lord.

Thought for the Day

Taste of the Lord and see that he is good.

June 3

Prayer for the Day

We are all born with a spark of the divine.
Father, I pray that I may tend the spark of the divine within me so that I may be gradually transformed from the old life to the new life.
Amen and thank you, Lord.

Thought for the Day

Doing the will of God will grow you in the will of God.

June 4

Prayer for the Day

I look around at everything you created, Lord, and all things are marvelous. Human beings are the most marvelous of all your creations. My prayer for today is that we all live up to our full potential.

Amen and thank you, Lord.

Thought for the Day

Breathe. You got this!

June 5

Prayer for the Day

Father, here we are with a new day upon us. What shall we do? Shall we sing and make music to the Lord? Yes, let's do that. I pray today, God, that someone who needs you so desperately will ask you to come into their life.

Amen and thank you, Lord.

Thought for the Day

It's not about where you've been but all about where you're going!

June 6

Prayer for the Day

Father, in your arms I have found I can be comforted when nothing else could comfort me. In your arms I found a place to rest. I do grow weary; we all do, but I'll always remember your arms. My prayer for today is that another weary soldier remembers those outstretched arms. Amen and thank you, Lord.

Thought for the Day

*When I wake up in the land of glory, to the saints
I will tell my story; there will be one name that
I proclaim! Jesus! La, la, la, la, la, la, la.*

June 7

Prayer for the Day

Father, I really want to do you a good job here on earth. I like to do things that I know will please you. I like to help people and be good to them, so this is my prayer for the day. Lord, keep my ear inclined to listen out for my next job and help me to perform these jobs with a smile.

Amen and thank you, Lord.

Thought for the Day

If I'm not doing a good job, I guess you'll have to take it up with my boss.

June 8

Prayer for the Day

Very quietly God speaks through your thoughts and feelings. Heed the divine voice of your conscience. Listen for this, and you will never be disappointed in the results of your life. Listen for this small still voice, and your tired nerves will be rested.

I pray that I may listen for the small still voice of God. I pray that I may obey the leading of my conscience.

Amen and thank you, Lord.

Thought for the Day

Your moral strength derives its effectiveness from the power that comes when you listen patiently for the small still voice.

June 9

Prayer for the Day

Father, I know of nothing sweeter than being asked to pray about someone or something. It is an honor and privilege to be able to bring my petitions or the petitions of others before you. That is trust, and I do not take it lightly.

My prayer for today is that others will reach out and ask for help when they or their loved ones need a touch from the Lord.

Amen and thank you, Lord.

Thought for the Day

Make this place a better world if you can. You can.

June 10

Prayer for the Day

Father, if we walk by sight instead of faith, we will continue on a path of disbelief and disappointment. It's not easy to give up control, especially when we're hurting and need relief, but I am not able to get the kind of results that last through the ages.

My prayer for today is that we all know without a shadow of a doubt that you will not fail us.

Amen and thank you, Lord.

Thought for the Day

Your ship may take on a little water, but if you believe and never doubt, you will not sink.

June 11

Prayer for the Day

Father, today is a brand-new day, and we are brand-new people. Gone is yesterday, and we won't worry about tomorrow. Today is a present, and I pray, Lord, we unwrap it with glee and anticipation.

Amen and thank you, Lord.

Thought for the Day

With a childlike approach, oh how we believe!

June 12

Prayer for the Day

Father, I believe in love, the kind of love that sustains life in hard times. I pray today that I can give love and receive love unconditionally.
Amen and thank you, Lord.

Thought for the Day

Yes, I believe in love. I believe most people are good.

June 13

Prayer for the Day

Father, a great awakening is upon us, and we live in a blessed land. May peace spread her wings far and wide, and may we all take steps to ensure that no one is left behind.
Amen and thank you, Lord.

Thought for the Day

I know you are tired, but don't you give up. Don't you dare give up. Your breakthrough is on the way!

June 14

Prayer for the Day

Father, we know what to do; we just don't always do *it*. Did we fail? Only if we fail to try again. My prayer for today is no matter how dark the hour, no matter how bad things seem that we will always remember and never forget that you, the Master of the wind, will not take your eyes off our life.

Amen and thank you, Lord.

Thought for the Day

It's nice to be important. It's more important to be nice. Just be nice.

June 15

Prayer for the Day

Father, great is thy faithfulness. Your mercy is anew each day. Knowing these two things help me face each day even when I don't feel like it.

My prayer for today is that we not put off for tomorrow what we are led to do today.

Amen and thank you, Lord.

Thought for the Day

We will all struggle. It's what we do next that determines our future.

June 16

Prayer for the Day

Father, our hope is secure when it is aligned with your desires for us. Disappointment with you occurs when our expectations do not coincide with your plan.

My prayer for today is to know without fail that the key to contentment and joy lie in placing all our personal hopes under the guidance of you.

Amen and thank you, Lord.

Thought for the Day

*On my own, I can change things only for a while.
My prayers can change things forever.*

June 17

Prayer for the Day

Father, being dependent upon you does not mean giving up my independence; it means that I will do well to place my hope where it is safe.
Amen and thank you, Lord.

Thought for the Day

Stand on your faith.

June 18

Prayer for the Day

Father, there's so much on my heart and mind today, full of emotions. My prayer for today is to remember you are a good, good Father, and I couldn't mess up bad enough to ever make you stop loving me.

Amen and thank you, Lord.

Thought for the Day

We are not perfect, but he is perfect in all of his ways.

June 19

Prayer for the Day

Father, we're living in a world that is hurting. We don't know their struggle, so we can't assume to know their pain.

My prayer for today is that we all lift one another up in prayer. It's what works. Amen and thank you, Lord.

Thought for the Day

Being kind doesn't cost a thing, but the *payday* is real.

June 20

Prayer for the Day

Father, we thank you for all we have. My prayer for today is to be grateful, be humble, and most of all, to be kind.
Amen and thank you, Lord.

Thought for the Day

Little things mean a lot.

June 21

Prayer for the Day

Father, good morning from your loved ones! We know how good you are, but we don't realize what good we can do.
My prayer for today is that we lay claim to what we want in life without disbelief. Amen and thank you, Lord.

Thought for the Day

Don't let what you see in the natural world cloud your vision. All things are possible.

June 22

Prayer for the Day

Father, no two days are the same, yet we serve an unchanging God. The way we view ourselves is not the way God views us, so even when we mess up—and we will mess up—he is still the same loving Father. He's always been.

My prayer for today is we lighten up on ourselves and forgive ourselves as the Father has.

Amen and thank you, Lord.

Thought for the Day

Each day is a fresh start, a new beginning.

June 23

Prayer for the Day

Father, I guess being overwhelmed comes with life. If I'm doing all I can, that's all anyone could ask for, so why is it that I allow my emotions to rule me? Breathe.

My prayer for today is that I abide in your rest, Lord. Amen and thank you, Lord.

Thought for the Day

Breathe in. Breathe out. Repeat.

June 24

Prayer for the Day

Father, I know that confusion comes from the enemy, and as long as the believers are confused, we go in circles. I don't want to go in circles. I want to be clear minded and approach that throne with confidence.

My prayer for today is that we walk boldly in our salvation. It did not come without a price.

Amen and thank you, Lord.

Thought for the Day

With every act of obedience, there comes a blessing.

June 25

Prayer for the Day

Father, what I think and how I think is not how you think. Your ways are so much higher than I can imagine.

My prayer for today is that I can rest in your idea of rest. Amen and thank you, Lord.

Thought for the Day

Trust the process.

June 26

Prayer for the Day

Father, we know you delivered us from bondage. If we have a desire for healing and trusting with total obedience, we know we can come before you boldly, knowing your love extends to us all.

My prayer for today is that whatever burden we're trying to shoulder alone will be laid at the foot of the cross not to be picked up again.

Amen and thank you, Lord.

Thought for the Day

He specializes in tough cases.

June 27

Prayer for the Day

Father, good morning from the one you love. Consider bread broken. We ask for your blessing upon it; much like when we're broken, we ask you to bless us. I take authority over my burdens and lift them to the great I Am! On my own, I will stay broken, but with you, I can do all things.

My prayer for today is that we rebuke sadness and darkness that has come to steal all joy.

Amen and thank you, Lord.

Thought for the Day

Even though I think he's not moving, he's already moved.

June 28

Prayer for the Day

Father, thank you for mercy, the rescue for our soul. My prayer for today is that we recognize when mercy walks in. Amen and thank you, Lord.

Thought for the Day

To show mercy is to show love.

June 29

Prayer for the Day

Father, thank you for the blessing of life. My prayer for today is to always be grateful and humble. Amen and thank you, Lord.

Thought for the Day

*Each day brings new opportunities.
Relish these new beginnings.*

June 30

Prayer for the Day

Father, some days I wake up and feel on top of the world. Some days I feel like my world is on top of me. No matter what I feel like, he knows where I am. I like that about God.

My prayer for today is that we can grasp that we have hope in Jesus, and we can rest assured. He is always the same.

Amen and thank you, Lord.

Thought for the Day

Stay faithful. It may seem like things will never change, but you can't go on how you feel. Go with what you know!

July 1

Prayer for the Day

Father, thank you for the Word. It is without a doubt a navigation system for the road of life. My prayer for today is that when we think we are without direction, we read the instructions. Amen and thank you, Lord.

Thought for the Day

When all else fails, read the instructions.

July 2

Prayer for the Day

Father, I wish things were different for people in tough situations, but until they're willing to change, all I can do is pray.

For today my prayer is that for every heartbreak anyone goes through that they are able to learn from it and accept that things can and will get better if they only will trust the Master.

Amen and thank you, Lord.

Thought for the Day

I am so humbled by the goodness our Lord and Savior has shown.

July 3

Prayer for the Day

Father, I know life is not as hard as I believe it to be. Too much has happened in such a short time, and it takes a toll on your mind-set and shoulders. I want to be happy again and be the person I once was. My prayer for today is that I allow you to love me.

Thought for the Day

I'm headed for a breakthrough. I know God knows where I am. I know he loves me.

July 4

Prayer for the Day

Father, thank you for all the freedom we enjoy, especially the freedom to worship. I'm glad it doesn't take a fifth to enjoy the fourth anymore. Everybody enjoy safely.

My prayer for today is that we can truly appreciate all we have. Amen and thank you, Lord.

Thought for the Day

It's a great day to be alive. We're free and not bound by any chains.

July 5

Prayer for the Day

Father, it's good to spend time with my sister. She looks up to me and always has. My prayer for today is that I always do my best to deserve that kind of respect from her. My prayer also is that you will bless her.

Amen and thank you, Lord.

Thought for the Day

Always be on your best behavior. Someone is watching and needs to have a role model.

July 6

Prayer for the Day

Father, thank you for second chances. My prayer for today is that someone who needs you will ask for you by name. Amen and thank you, Lord.

Thought for the Day

Everyone deserves to be treated with respect.

July 7

Prayer for the Day

Lord, you know my burden, how heavy the load is. I can't help but wonder when things will change. I've been praying a long time about this that hangs around my neck like an albatross. I know you will do something to change this situation, and I'm okay with your decision.

Amen and thank you, Lord.

Thought for the Day

There is always something to be thankful about.

July 8

Prayer for the Day

Lord, I am thankful for those you place in my path. Out of the blue, you run into people that are fighting one of the same battles you are fighting, and you cry and hug and promise to pray for one another, random yet steps ordered by you, Lord.

It lets me know I am not the only one that struggles. Sometimes though, you think you're the only one; not for one minute am I glad anyone is struggling, but it was a reminder to be more kind, show more kindness, be more like you.

Amen and thank you, Lord.

Thought for the Day

Life may be but a few days, but the struggle is real. I'm going to praise him anyway.

July 9

Prayer for the Day

Father, I adore you, and you have been faithful. I pray that each day I draw breath I am faithful to you.
    Amen and thank you, Lord.

Thought for the Day

Moving myself out of his way allows him to move freely.

July 10

Prayer for the Day

Father, do I care too much, try so hard for others that they feel they don't have to try for themselves? I'm a long way from where I want to be, but I thank you, God, that I'm not where I used to be. From experience, I can say that until a person wants a better way of life, I can't want it for them and it happen. My life is not perfect, but at the end of the day, I bow my head to thank God for another day and ask him to forgive my sins. Life on this earth is fleeting, and you may have happiness, but joy is what lasts.

My prayer for this day, Lord, is to help us as we struggle along finding joy along life's way.

Amen and thank you, Lord.

Thought for the Day

There is joy in the journey once you realize you are not alone as you journey.

July 11

Prayer for the Day

Father, I thank you for the heart you instilled in me. I am loving and kind because of your grace and mercy. My desire is to mature in my faith, walk always trusting that you will lead me to my destination. I have cried out to you, Father, and you've heard my prayers. I know that I can trust you, and I trust you more as the days pass.

Amen and thank you, Lord.

Thought for the Day

Sometimes you have to do things that are unpleasant to rescue someone that doesn't know they need rescuing.

July 12

Prayer for the Day

Father, I see more every day that I am a mere mortal. I can change nothing on my own nor make others change, but I am resting on your promises, and they are infallible. The only guarantee in life is a promise you made your children, and that is you would never leave us nor forsake us. That promise keeps me going even when things look hopeless. Sure, we will have problems in life, but as a child of God, I will be part of the solution, not part of the problem.

Amen and thank you, Lord.

Thought for the Day

He knows my name.

July 13

Prayer for the Day

Father, to wake up is a blessing. To know I am able to do anything because of you strikes gratitude in my heart. Once I figured out that I didn't have to be perfect but knew the one that was, is, and always will be, it gets me through the day.

Resting in your arms poses no problems; it solves them. My prayer for today is to cruise with the top back. You are the wind that blows through my hair.

Amen and thank you, Lord.

Thought for the Day

The battle is not ours. He knew the ending before it began.

July 14

Prayer for the Day

Lord, his life is such a mess, and he doesn't even know how messy it is. I'll not pull out my good weapon. I'm pulling out my best weapon—our God. I pray he leans toward you, then on you. The streets are mean, and they get meaner by the day, yet that's where most of his time is spent. It's time to be a victor and not the victim. His beautiful season is here. I claim it.

Amen and thank you, Lord.

Thought for the Day

The sun is coming up. I know you have battled all night. Please rest now.

July 15

Prayer for the Day

Father, another day is on our doorstep, and we are blessed with our life. A lot can happen in a day and so much accomplished in a day. Praying from the heart to be a blessing to someone today, opening my mouth always to tell someone the good news. Praying for my pastor's anointing today and that the ears not only receive but the heart too. Asking you, Lord, to help me live in today, taking things one day at a time. It's all about you today, Father.

Amen and thank you, Lord.

Thought for the Day

This is the day that the Lord has made. Because of him, I will rejoice and be glad in it.

July 16

Prayer for the Day

Lord, I have so much to be thankful for, and you have truly blessed me. Today is a big day for me as I go to Day Report to carry the message of hope for those still suffering from addiction. I pray your words come from my lips to touch a heart to reveal there is a better way of life. The struggle is real.
    Amen and thank you, Lord.

Thought for the Day

Little is much when God is in the midst.

July 17

Prayer for the Day

Lord, here we stand facing a new day; able we are. Capable we can because of your strength. Thank you that we don't have to depend on ourselves or go this life alone. I pray that we all realize the depth of mercy.

Amen and thank you, Lord.

Thought for the Day

When mercy walks in.
PS. I pray your day is filled with your heart's desire.

July 18

Prayer for the Day

Lord, I am giving my praise to you, for worthy is your name. No prayer requests, I'm asking for nothing. I just want to thank you for being so good to me.
Amen and thank you, Lord.

Thought for the Day

Worthy is the Lamb, without spot or blemish.

July 19

Prayer for the Day

Good morning, Father, and thank you for little children. Your word talks about little children in Matthew. Praying for all children to be taught about you so when they grow up they will be like you.

Amen and thank you, Lord.

Thought for the Day

Mistreat no one, especially the little ones.

July 20

Prayer for the Day

I am so thankful to be alive. I am striving to have less of me in everything and more of you. I pray to be a blessing to someone today, for I have truly been blessed. Amen and thank you, Lord.

Thought for the Day

When I realized he didn't expect me to be perfect, things became more manageable.

July 21

Prayer for the Day

No one you meet comes down your path on accident. Allow these people, who are not accidents, to witness to you, interact with you, encourage you.

My prayer for today is to always be grateful for everyone I see and to appreciate people, all people.

Amen and thank you, Lord.

Thought for the Day

People need other people. God made us to want interaction with others, but he wants us to interact with him more than anything!

July 22

Prayer for the Day

I love Sundays. It even feels different on a Son Day. Thank you for your peace. My prayer for today, Lord, I pray we rest in your peace.
 Amen and thank you, Lord.

Thought for the Day

Soak in his presence.

July 23

Prayer for the Day

Maybe you woke up burdened by the same troubles you laid down with. I have done that myself. Instead of shouldering the burden yourself, give it to the One that is able to change your burden into victory. Without him, we are just spinning our wheels. Ask him to help. He waits to hear us cry for him. I pray that today we can live in peace knowing that the burden is not ours.
Amen and thank you, Lord.

Thought for the Day

Even death could not hold him. If he can overcome death, just think what he can do for you!

July 24

Prayer for the Day

Lord, since none among us is perfect, we thank you for your grace. Each day brings its own set of challenges, but if we stick with the one that sticks with us closer than a brother, all will be well. If I can be a better person today than I was yesterday, I will be satisfied.

Amen and thank you, Lord.

Thought for the Day

Life is not always easy, but it is *doable*.
Keep your eye on the prize.

July 25

Prayer for the Day

Lord, here another day has come for us. No matter what our plans are, Lord, you are the ultimate decider on what we will accomplish. Whatever we do today, we want to work at it with our whole heart, bringing glory to your name.

Amen and thank you, Lord.

Thought for the Day

In a world where you can be anything you want, why not be yourself?

July 26

Prayer for the Day

Lord, I know you do not excuse our sin. I know you are a loving heavenly Father and that you will use discipline to bring us back to godly behavior. I know you allow us to experience the consequences of sin, but I know divine condemnation is not one of them.

Amen and thank you, Lord.

Thought for the Day

Won't you open your heart and mind to receive God's love today?

July 27

Prayer for the Day

Lord, I guess the mornings are the most peaceful for me. Early in the day, everyone is still asleep; only the birds are awake, and they're singing. They're happy, and they know seed is on the way. But, Lord, what about other seeds? Am I sowing where you need me to? I know I can be a little hardheaded and talk too much, so if I talk less, will you talk to me more?

Amen and thank you, Lord.

Thought for the Day

Two ears one mouth.

July 28

Prayer for the Day

Lord, I wasn't excited about getting up at six this morning, but I am so excited to be going to Day Report to minister this morning! Something happened yesterday, and the devil told me I wasn't worthy enough to post a prayer today. I called him out on that and rebuked him in the name of Jesus!
    Amen and thank you, Lord.

Thought for the Day

Just because you mess up doesn't mean you are out of the game. It means learn from your mistake and try to do better. Love you and bless you!

July 29

Prayer for the Day

Lord, I sit this morning and admire your handiwork, and I know that we as a whole are so blessed. It's not good to take things or people for granted. Life can and will throw you some curveballs, but to give up is not an option. We've come so far, yet we have further to go. We don't have to go it alone. There is hope, and Jesus is his name.

Amen and thank you, Lord.

Thought for the Day

How will you ever know if you can hit a homer in if you don't step up and take a swing?

July 30

Prayer for the Day

Lord, thank you for my family and friends. They are the cheerleaders for me in this game called *keeping it right*. Sometimes we have fun, and sometimes we have to handle business and get down to business! There are so many people that need a kind word, our prayers, our encouragement. I want to be a person that you feel comfortable asking me to pray for you, or if it's serious, you know I'll take it seriously. Lord, I'm just looking to grow a little more every day and step into my beautiful season but also help someone else step into their beautiful season.

With God, nothing is impossible. This is truth. Amen and thank you, Lord.

Thought for the Day

Be a blessing to someone today.

July 31

Prayer for the Day

Lord, I thank you for believing in me when I didn't believe in myself. No one thought I'd ever amount to anything, yet here I am on top of the world and loving life. A heartfelt thanks to those who cheered me on through my journey and people that you placed in my path. I wouldn't trade any of the yesterdays for all of my tomorrows. There were times that I was doing pretty good, but I didn't know the full extent of what you had planned for me. When you showed up, you showed out, Lord. I shouldn't be here, yet I am, and that tells me my work here is not finished. I have an inner peace that I let get lost amongst the chaos sometimes, but at the end of the day, I'm still standing, praising God, and looking to improve daily.

Amen and thank you, Lord.

Thought for the Day

I'm still crazy but at least I am no longer insane!

August 1

Prayer for the Day

Father, we don't like giving up destructive behaviors because it is painful, and the changes required for recovery are often specially painful. Some would rather suffer in a known situation than risk moving into the unknown world of recovery. My prayer today is that every addict that is suffering will find the courage to step out of their comfort zone straight into the arms of our loving and forgiving Father.
    Amen and thank you, Lord.

Thought for the Day

Our growth involves some pain, but we can be confident that the sacrifices we make will be ultimately worthwhile. Knowing that there will be hard times in recovery can help us face them and persevere in the healing process.

August 2

Prayer for the Day

Father, we all learn from our parents and pass on the lessons we learned, good or bad, to our children. We blame our parents for our character defects and weep because we have passed those same defects on to our children. We can stop the cycle of passing destructive traits from one generation to the next by turning our life over to God. As we obey God, we will model a transformed life to our children. As they see the power of our vibrant faith in God, they will be likely to follow in our steps.

Amen and thank you, Lord.

Thought for the Day

You cannot ever be too far for God to reach you. You have to want him to; that is, you must be willing to change.

August 3

Prayer for the Day

Father, in Jesus's Name, I see from your Word that you were willing to give of yourself in the person of your Son for all men. I understand because Jesus is Lord of my life. I, too, am called to give myself to others. I choose to accept that calling today. I'll give of my time. I'll give of your love in me. I'll be strong and lift up those who are weak. I'm willing to be available to be used of you so that those around me might experience the abundant life you have provided. You have loved me, Lord, with the greatest love there is. I count it a privilege now to share that love with others.

Amen and thank you, Lord.

Thought for the Day

A burden shared is a burden halved.

August 4

Prayer for the Day

Father, as I sit in my chair, my altar surrounded by all my studies of your Word, that is a time of reflection. Many people come to my mind from the past, like ghosts whispering in the night. Many did not make it out of their addiction. I did, and I only know that your purpose for me on earth, my mission, must be very important. Lead me, Lord, to be where I need to be, doing the things I need to do, for I am willing. I serve a mighty God, and I wouldn't trade what I feel now for the way I felt then for all the drugs in the world. This is a feeling like none I've ever known, and no amount of money can buy it. Praise God.

Amen and thank you, Lord.

Thought for the Day

I will always remember the past, but I will never repeat it.

August 5

Prayer for the Day

Father, we know that Satan sends the spirit of division among us. He knows that a house divided against itself will fall. He also knows that if we all come together in the unity of our faith, we'll arrive at the full stature of Christ Jesus, so he has assigned a spirit of division to operate in our personal life, our church life, our social life, and in our family life. We don't have to yield to that spirit. By speaking the truth in love, we will grow up into him in all things, which the head is Jesus Christ.

Amen and thank you, Lord.

Thought for the Day

Envying, strife, and division will reduce you back to a carnal state of mind.

August 6

Prayer for the Day

Father, giving and receiving forgiveness is an essential part of our present healing. This requires that we make peace with God, within ourselves, and others whom we have alienated. Once we go through the process of making amends, we must keep our mind and our heart open to anyone we may have overlooked. God will often remind us of relationships that need attention. When these come to mind, we should stop everything and go to those we have offended and seek to repair the damage. Lord, I pray to always be obedient.

Amen and thank you, Lord.

Thought for the Day

There is hope for all of us no matter how terrible our past or the problems we face today.

August 7

Prayer for the Day

Father, we may feel deep insecurities and hurt over the abuse, misunderstandings, and injustices we have suffered at the hands of others. Our hope is in you, God, who will come again and rule the world in justice and truth. You, Lord, will straighten out all the inequities of the past. When your kingdom is established, we will not have anything to fear. Nothing will hurt or destroy in all God's holy mountain.

Amen and thank you, Lord.

Thought for the Day

If our family is broken because of addiction, jealousy, or any other thing of hindrance, God can unify and heal it.

August 8

Prayer for the Day

Father, our sins do not affect only us; they affect our family, our friends, our nation, and even our planet. It is sobering to realize that what we do has such a great impact on the world. Our whole country is suffering the effects of alcoholism, drug addiction, infidelity, etc., and these problems seem to be getting worse. Recovery is important to us and our loved ones, but there is even more at stake than we realize. If each of us would successfully complete the recovery program, dependency and addiction would decline, and sobriety would benefit and begin a recovery process of its own. There is one who holds hope in his hand. I pray our people will turn to the one that loved them before they were formed in their mother's womb.

Amen and thank you, Lord.

Thought for the Day

There is no condemnation in Christ.

August 9

Prayer for the Day

Father, I love to praise your name and give you my uninhibited praise. I used to be a little shy about getting loud and getting down at church, but the place that I go to worship invites us to praise however we want to. I am blessed with a family of brothers and sisters that do not look at me funny. My prayer is that everyone would feel that spirit upon them wherever they are and let loose. It's a freedom like I've never known.

Amen and thank you, Lord.

Thought for the Day

Courage isn't the absence of fear. Courage means we take advantage of the little strength we find within ourselves, enough strength to take the next step.

August 10

Prayer for the Day

Father, for years we have heard that we are living in the end-times, and when we look around, it's easy to believe that. My Bible tells me that this world is still standing because it is your desire to not see anyone perish to miss out on the kingdom that awaits. My fervent prayer for today is that we as Christians *double down* in our efforts to get the good news of the gospel to as many as possible. We are living proof that there is a God and that he can and will change lives. Our testimony is the greatest indication of a true and living God.

  Amen and thank you, Lord.

Thought for the Day

God will reward our efforts if we are fully committed to following his will and prove it by our actions.
PS. Don't keep all the wonderful things the Lord has done for you to yourself. These things were meant to be shared.

August 11

Prayer for the Day

Father, each one of us has a valuable story to tell. We may feel shy and awkward about speaking. We may think that what we have to say is too trivial. Is it actually going to help anyone else? We may struggle to get beyond the shame of our past experiences, but our recovery story can help others who are trapped back where we used to be. Are we willing to allow God to use us to help free others? My prayer is that we are willing to be a vessel for God to work through.
Amen and thank you, Lord.

Thought for the Day

When people hear our story, we are offering them the chance to loosen their chains and begin their own recovery.

August 12

Prayer for the Day

Father, in the Bible it talks about peace that surpasses all understanding. That very thing is my heart's desire, and I know that I, in fact, do not yet have this kind of peace. My prayer today, Lord, is that we all would begin a journey that brings us to that place where it's not necessary to know but so essential to a place of rest.
    Amen and thank you, Lord.

Thought for the Day

Diligence in prayer will bring about many things in life, and prayer insists that you trust him enough to lay it down.

August 13

Prayer for the Day

Father, I bring my praise to you. I have seen and felt things in the last two days, really a miracle. I've been praying a long time about this. Forgive me, Lord, that I ever doubted your faithfulness. When I could not even speak aloud, you heard the utterances of my heart. I came to that crossroad of life that all believers will come to; can you really and truly lay it down and find the peace and joy you have been searching for, or do you keep trying to be the captain of your own ship? I will never be able to navigate the course without my Lord and Savior.

Amen and thank you, Lord.

Thought for the Day

The Apostle Paul shows us in Romans chapter 6 how to open the successful Christian life with four key words: know, reckon, yield, and obey. The Christian can conquer sin because Christ lives in us.

August 14

Prayer for the Day

Father, all of us have our own battle to win, the battle between the material view of life and the spiritual view. We can choose good or evil, but we cannot choose both. I pray, Lord, that I may choose the good and resist the evil. I will not be a loser in the battle for righteousness.

Amen and thank you, Lord.

Thought for the Day

If we win the victory, we can believe that even God in his heaven will rejoice.

August 15

Prayer for the Day

Father, today is a fresh start, a chance to be better than we were yesterday. I still struggle with things I've prayed to overcome. That is flesh, and we will all make mistakes, but what I am most grateful for is that God allows me a chance to work on these things by the opening of my eyes to a new day. In my weakness I cried out to my Father, and in his strength he answers me. You're a good, good Father. It's who you are.

Amen and thank you, Lord.

Thought for the Day

I don't know what tomorrow holds, but I do know who holds tomorrow, the great I Am. You are perfect in all of your ways, and I am loved by you.

August 16

Prayer for the Day

Father, our strength is found in you and you alone, ever present, a refuge from the storms of life. Amen and thank you, Lord.

Thought for the Day

Life, the more things change, the more they stay the same.

August 17

Prayer for the Day

Lord, I am praying for all the little babies in the hospital. They are so pure and innocent, and we live in a world that takes that innocence quickly unless we continue to be foot soldiers for the kingdom of Christ. Babies are God's miracle to the world, and every time a baby is born, hope is born too. Yes, babies need us, but we need them to keep us on course.

Amen and thank you, Lord.

Thought for the Day

Babies keep us mindful of our own helplessness.

August 18

Prayer for the Day

Father, I am so thankful that you loved me enough not to leave me broken, and in my mess, I know I'll make mistakes throughout my life. I know I'll never be perfect, but what I do know is that you love me. I think the last year has been one of the worst I've ever known for several different reasons and that I have doubted my mountain could be moved, but you are a God that takes the impossible and makes it possible. You said never would you put more on us than we could bear. I'm carrying all I think I can, Lord. I pray for a light at the end of my tunnel. I know I'm impatient and think you're slow to move, but that is not my place to try and move you. It is my place to remain faithful, remembering always what a mighty God I serve.

Amen and thank you, Lord.

Thought for the Day

When you've done all you can to stand, kneel.

August 19

Prayer for the Day

Father, through it all, you are steadfast and never wavering. No matter what season of my life I was going through, I knew there was a God, and I knew that he loved me. That is an unconditional love that no man will ever be able to provide. Lord, I believe I am being prepared to step into the next season of my life. I will embrace it. Thank you for all my fiery trials; it made me who I am today but still a work in progress.

Amen and thank you, Lord.

Thought for the Day

Lord, prepare me for sanctuary.

August 20

Prayer for the Day

Father, I thank you for the life in me. I praise you because worthy is the Lamb. Life is not a bed of roses, but I know you are always watching over me and mine. Let me gain the strength and wisdom to never lose my moral compass again, always to do my best to be pleasing unto thy sight.

Amen and thank you, Lord.

Thought for the Day

A lot of people walk with their head down. Look up! That's where the store room of heaven is, and you have not because you ask not.

August 21

Prayer for the Day

Father, I have love in my heart and always so willing to show love. Why at a time when I need to show love do I show the side of me that does not portray love? Tempers, angry words—they both hurt, and I grieve over what can't be unsaid or undone. The only thing that would soothe me was to fall on my knees. Yes, I felt like they were being slick, and they had no right, but at the end of the day, it only hurt me. They went on without a thought. I pray for these two people and especially the one that is too small to take care of himself.

Amen and thank you, Lord.

Thought for the Day

*I'm so glad he isn't finished with me yet.
I still need lots of work.*

August 22

Prayer for the Day

Father, I'll never question you why, although sometimes I do wonder. I don't have to roll on the ground like David and beat my chest and beg for a blessing. What I will do, Lord, is to remain rooted firmly and faithfully in hope. I know, I mean, I really know that what God puts in place will be perfect because his timing is perfect. When his plan unfolds, I will have peace. I strive now. I won't always.

Amen and thank you, Lord.

Thought for the Day

I'm gonna keep the faith and rope the hope!

August 23

Prayer for the Day

Father, thank you that you can be everywhere all at once, watching the people going through this horrible hurricane. I know you are in control of this situation, and I'm sure the victims know, but can you for one moment imagine how they feel? I pray, Lord, to always feel the pain of others so that I will be diligent about praying for others. Bless them, Lord, and keep them as I know you will. Amen and thank you, Lord.

Thought for the Day

Everybody can't do everything, but everybody can do something. As Christians, we have the power to move mountains with our prayers.

August 24

Prayer for the Day

Father, another day has come for us. Praise God, we have the opportunity to be better than we were yesterday. I am heartbroken for those who are going through Hurricane Harvey but comforted knowing you are with them to comfort and soothe. God, I know you know right where each person is and what they need. I praise your name. Holy, holy, holy.
    Amen and thank you, Lord.

Thought for the Day

There will be storms in our life.
He will not forsake nor leave us.

August 25

Prayer for the Day

Father, sometimes we don't think we deserve any better, but you gave your best so we would have the best. Even if you're scared, you have to try to make your situation better. Misery does love company, but aren't you tired of being miserable?
Amen and thank you, Lord.

Thought for the Day

Be your number 1 cheer leader.

August 26

Prayer for the Day

Father, what we know now is not complete, so we will always wonder why, when, or how. It's our nature. I am working so hard to have the kind of faith that will not waver no matter the storm. Lord, I know you do not slumber nor rest. In the late-night hours you, Lord, are working on our behalf, making intercession to God for us. I do make sure to say, "Thy will be done," when I pray. I have accepted and conformed my mind to never doubt; my God always knows what is best for me for all of us. I'm not in charge. He is. Whew. I was tired.

Amen and thank you, Lord.

Thought for the Day

Learn to lean on self less and him more.
He wants us to let him do his job.

August 27

Prayer for the Day

Father, there's not a rock in this world that I would let take my place in praising you! I will praise you until I leave this earth, and when that day comes, I will get to praise you in my heavenly home! When your heart is so full that you feel like you're just going to bust wide open, you're full of the love of God. So as some of you have already suspected, I'm full of it. Yes, full of praise and thankfulness for my Lord and Master. My prayer for today is to share the light that has so thoroughly lit my path with a brother or sister that is looking and searching for what they need. I can do this, Lord, because I am the daughter of the King!

Amen and thank you, Lord.

Thought for the Day

There is hope. There is always hope.

August 28

Prayer for the Day

Father, here we are at the dawning of a new day, a fresh start. Opportunity awaits, and life unfolds. Asking for help does not mean we don't know what to do; it means we know the one that can help us do it best. Thank you for never leaving us nor forsaking us no matter what mess we got ourselves into. You are a good, good Father. It's who you are. My prayer for today is that we humble ourselves before you and recognize just how much power is in the blood.

Amen and thank you, Lord.

Thought for the Day

Didn't he always show up right on time?

August 29

Prayer for the Day

Father, when we commit all our plans to you, we will succeed. It says so in Psalms. That is reassuring when we face things that seem so uncertain! I am who you say I am. I can do what you say I can do. Whew. Rest with this today, children of God. My prayer for today is that we will rest in your love and faithfulness.

Amen and thank you, Lord.

Thought for the Day

One day at a time, that's all we should focus on.
No one knows what tomorrow will bring.

August 30

Prayer for the Day

Father, early morning I feel the most alive. It's still and quiet, and my mediation with you humbles me for the day. It is in this time that I can tell you all I feel and have you shower me with your love. You are preparing me to face the day ahead without worry or fear. My prayer for today is that someone with a love for you will show a brother or sister in need what it means to give it to the Lord.

Amen and thank you, Lord.

Thought for the Day

Grace. It even sounds good to the ear.
Imagine how much better it feels!

August 31

Prayer for the Day

Father, how long I have prayed for him. How many sleepless nights I have endured. I got a phone call last night that caused me to break down and sob. He told me he's been in the book of James and began to quote scripture to me, and my hopes and dreams came alive once more. There's nothing a parent wants any more than to see their child's life come to fruition.

My prayer for today is that he will begin to understand all that God has for him and that there is so much more to life. I pray this for your children as well. God bless our prayers, and, Lord, thank you. Amen.

Thought for the Day

Pray without ceasing.

September 1

Prayer for the Day

Heavenly Father, thank you for another day as none are promised. I often wonder when this heavy load I'm dragging will at least ease up. On this earth, we will shoulder heavy burdens, and I know we all have our fair share and how glad I am to know one day after a while that all of these worldly burdens will end. Thank you for not leaving me in my mess.

Amen and thank you, Lord.

Thought for the Day

I can do all things through Christ who strengthens me.

September 2

Prayer for the Day

Heavenly Father, every Sunday morning, Satan does his best to keep me from church. I almost fell for it, Lord, again. God, I pray to be an overcomer of anything that separates me from you. Amen and thank you, Lord.

Thought for the Day

May nothing keep us from him.

September 3

Prayer for the Day

Heavenly Father, thank you for another day. I pray to be a good servant today, willing to listen to that small still voice that guides my life. I pray, Lord, to be a light that shines in a dark world. There is something in all of us that yearns to be good and do good. Let us follow through with our good intentions.

Amen and thank you, Lord.

Thought for the Day

Is your light shining today?

September 4

Prayer for the Day

Father, here we stand at the dawning of a new day, and we're going to need your help. We are weak and tired but made strong in you. We will sing and make music to you today in our heart no matter where we are! We can do that, and no matter what is swirling around us, be at rest even though we are hard at work.

My prayer for today is we will never forget that we are equipped to not only get through the day but seize the day!

Amen and thank you, Lord.

Thought for the Day

It's all in who you know.

September 5

Prayer for the Day

Father, sometimes I feel like a donut, all fluffy around the edges but hollow in the middle. I need to fill up again! I sang a song in my head all day yesterday. "My hero is coming to my rescue." I needed to hear that song on Sunday from the praise team. I get filled up on Sunday. Why can't every day be like Sunday, Lord?

My prayer for today is that we can let his blessings flow through us and let our light shine brighter than yesterday.

Amen and thank you, Lord.

Thought for the Day

He is the rescue for my soul.

September 6

Prayer for the Day

Father, we know we are to pray without ceasing. All day I find myself singing praise songs or having conversations with you. I feel better when we talk, Lord. Thank you for having my back at all times. I don't know what I would do without you. Don't know where I'd be.

My prayer for today is that we take hold of your hand and walk with you through life.

Amen and thank you, Lord.

Thought for the Day

Take his hand and allow yourself to be led.

September 7

Prayer for the Day

Father, your Word says, "I will refresh the weary and satisfy the faint." That's good news this morning as my body is tired, and my bones ache. I have always said I don't work for the glory of man but for the glory of God. When I work with this thought, I can do anything and not feel like giving up.

My prayer for today is that we cry unto the one that makes us whole and will see us through from start to finish.

Amen and thank you, Lord.

Thought for the Day

I love all days that end in y, but today is Friday. Woohoo!

September 8

Prayer for the Day

Father, most of us would agree that suffering is one of the most difficult parts of life to accept, much less understand. All of us suffer, and suffering is a part of life. We must accept that we will hurt from time to time. God, we know you equip us to live at peace in the midst of tough times. My prayer for today is that we hold fast to Christ and live according to his will. Amen and thank you, Lord.

Thought for the Day

Tough times don't last. Tough folks do. Hold on.

September 9

Prayer for the Day

Father, I always heard there were only two things certain, death and taxes, but that's not true. You are certain and unchangeable. You are not like shifting shadows that change but sure and true in all your ways. Isaiah 26:4 says, "Trust in the Lord forever, for the Lord, the Lord is the Rock eternal."

My prayer for today is that we hold fast to the truth, the true and living God that will sustain and keep us. I as well pray your day is blessed and peaceful, my friend.

Amen and thank you, Lord.

Thought for the Day

Our foot is on the rock, and our name is on the roll! Yeah. We gonna rock 'n' roll!

September 10

Prayer for the Day

Father, another day has come for us. What a blessing. What we choose to do with it is up to us. Living in the now is hard sometimes since we're so intent on worrying about tomorrow. Doesn't it hold enough worry all on its own? Focus on today.

My prayer for today is that we live in today, doing our very best with you as our ever-present help.

Amen and thank you, Lord.

Thought for the Day

Live, laugh, love. It's going to be all right.

September 11

Prayer for the Day

Father, this date lives in our hearts and minds forever as a day that rocked our sense of security. The terror and pain we watched will always make us remember that we have so much love for our brothers and sisters, and we are willing to reach out and help not just in a crisis but always because of the way you put us together.

My prayer for today is that we never get too big for our britches. Remember, we all put our pants on one leg at a time. I pray your day is filled with peace and joy as you walk through this life.

Amen and thank you, Lord.

Thought for the Day

Faith, hope, and love—the greatest is love.

September 12

Prayer for the Day

Father, this world is addicted to activity. We seem to always need to be doing something. You tell us to be at rest with you and meditate quietly. Your Word says, "Peace I leave with you; my peace I give you. I do not give to you as the world gives. Do not let your hearts be troubled and do not be afraid." Words to live by and this, Lord, is my prayer for today. May we soak in your peace.
Amen and thank you, Lord.

Thought for the Day

Living close to him is a sure defense against evil.

September 13

Prayer for the Day

Father, I am just a lump of clay, and you are the potter. If I am this or that, it's because you are working on me each and every day. Sometimes I resist and try things on my own in my own way. Thank you, Lord, that your mercies are new each day.

My prayer for today is to trust the process and realize that we are being refined in the fire. Amen and thank you, Lord.

Thought for the Day

I can be anything at all. I was created by the Master.

September 14

Prayer for the Day

Father, let me be humble. Let me be ever so humble.

Thought for the Day

I fail. I fall. I rise. I fly.

September 15

Prayer for the Day

Father, we know a season is not measured in years but rather in a time of its own. I know I have had several seasons in my life, and they all are meant to bring about your purpose. Sometimes it's not pleasant, but always I feel needful.

My prayer for today is that we recognize no matter where or what we're going through that it is but a season.

Hey, guys, I love you, and I pray you have a blessed day! Amen and thank you, Lord.

Thought for the Day

Your beautiful season is upon you.

September 16

Prayer for the Day

Father, I imagine what heaven is like, and I know it's glorious and beautiful, but I also imagine that there are storehouses of blessings with our name on them. How good is that?

My prayer for today is that in all our ways we will be stable, resting on the promises of God and asking in faith for what we need. Amen and thank you, Lord.

Thought for the Day

We have not because we asked not.

September 17

Prayer for the Day

Father, we are all looking for our *true north*. We can make all the plans we want, but it is only with your direction that we will get there. Remembering that life is but a vapor may help, unless we are truly determined to go it on our own. Your ways and thoughts are so much higher than mine that what I think is good may really be only mediocre to you.

My prayer for today is that we learn to live each and every day constantly asking, "What is your will, Father?"

Amen and thank you, Lord.

Thought for the Day

No matter what I do or accomplish, the Father first ordained those steps. Hey y'all, let's get it!

September 18

Prayer for the Day

Father, I ask myself throughout the day, *Am I pleasing to my Lord? Am I walking in his ways, or am I trying to walk my own way?* I've always said that no matter what you do, do it as if the Lord is watching. (He is.) Concerning your job, work to please the Lord; work for the glory of God, not man.

My prayer for today is that we grasp the imparted knowledge that God loves us, and he will see us through. Seek first the kingdom, and all else will be added to you.

Amen and thank you, Lord.

Thought for the Day

Humble pie, mmm, good!

September 19

Prayer for the Day

Father, my body is tired, but you're not. Depending on this strength, the strength that comes from you is what I'll be depending on today. I keep thinking of Ezekiel 37:1–10 and the dry bones that came to life. Thinking about this encourages me to keep moving.

My prayer for today is that we all truly grasp that where we are, there you'll be. Amen and thank you, Lord.

Thought for the Day

We just gotta keep slugging at it. We have a helper. His name is Jesus.

September 20

Prayer for the Day

Father, I am an imperfect person living in an imperfect world, but I have hope that comes only from a relationship with you. Thank you for loving me.

My prayer for today is that no matter what we do or don't do that we realize you knew from the beginning we would not get it right every time.

Amen and thank you, Lord.

Thought for the Day

Hold your head up, child of God!

September 21

Prayer for the Day

Father, my aunt bought me a 365-day journal by Sarah Young titled *Jesus Calling (Enjoying Peace in His Presence)*, and it is a wonderful read early in the morning before I start my day. It's as if you yourself are speaking. Before the demands of the day assail me, I sit and read this journal. It sustains and strengthens my very soul. My aunt has been a wonderful addition to our family for many, many years, and so today my prayer is for her and her family.

Father, I pray that you will strengthen her when she is weak and the demands of life seem overwhelming. Thank you for her love and care for her precious family. I pray that for many generations to come her family will be strong and true to you, Father.

Amen and thank you, Lord.

Thought for the Day

*In the morning, O Lord, you hear my voice;
in the morning, I lay my requests before you and
wait in expectation (Psalm 5:3).*

September 22

Prayer for the Day

Father, I understand that human beings are the only creatures you created that can anticipate future events. That is a blessing and a curse! Let us not worry about anything and think on the lovely and good!

My prayer for today is that no matter what we think we have to worry about, that instead we give it up, letting go of the burden so that walking by faith instead of sight is the normal.

Amen and thank you, Lord.

Thought for the Day

Though heaven is future, it is also present tense. As you walk in the light with me, you have one foot on earth and one foot in heaven.

September 23

Prayer for the Day

Father, I am blessed, so blessed. I have a biological family and a church family that love me despite my imperfections. I have everything I need to succeed in life and the promises of a loving God. It doesn't get any better than that.

My prayer for today is that we count our blessings before we begin to grumble, and that will keep us thankful.

Amen and thank you, Lord.

Thought for the Day

What we have in life is not left to chance as long as we depend on the Father. He will sustain us.

September 24

Prayer for the Day

Father, the mind is willing, but the body betrays us. Mother told me before she passed that her body betrayed her. I know what she meant. I am tired, and my bones hurt this morning, so I know I need your help, Lord. Getting old is not for sissies. I see, but I'm going to give this day my best.

My prayer for today is that we ask for all things in Jesus's name, calling to him to hold us up and sustain us.

Amen and thank you, Lord.

Thought for the Day

Wish I known then what I for sure know now.

September 25

Prayer for the Day

Father, the rain comes down, and it is soothing to listen to. Whatever worries, my soul can be soothed when I sit quietly with you. I cannot be swayed by the glitter and glam of this world, for I was already bought and paid for by a price so great that the sheer enormity of it makes me sob with joy. We should always remember your work at the cross when our lives seem to be spiraling out of control. Man does not fully appreciate what you did because you loved us so much.

My prayer for today is that we will remember the cross and how even though you were so badly, horribly, inhumanly treated, you went anyway.

Now that is love. That is love unconditionally. Amen and thank you, Lord.

Thought for the Day

Give it all you've got. He did. He surely did.

September 26

Prayer for the Day

Father, this morning, I feel peaceful and oh so blessed. I hear the crickets, and they are peaceful and soothing. In a little while, life will be so different. Job demands; life demands. The list goes on. No matter what we're facing today, we have an advocate with you, and his name is Jesus. When you face trouble, whisper his name or shout it. Either way, he will hear you.

My prayer for today is that we never lose hope nor sight of who we are in him. Amen and thank you, Lord.

Thought for the Day

It's a beautiful morning. I think I'll just go and shine. Yeah, let's shine today!

September 27

Prayer for the Day

Father, I believe most people are good. Luke Bryan sings a song about it, and it always puts me in a positive frame of mind. I do try to see the best in everyone, giving them the opportunity to be a good friend because I make friends easily. I'm not shy when I meet you. I feel like we've been friends forever. Jesus teaches us about love because he loves us unconditionally. How can we not practice love?

My prayer for today is that we let loose and love others. I mean, show love, give love, be ready to receive love.

Amen and thank you, Lord.

PS. If no one has told you lately they love you, God loves you, and I love you. Have a beautiful day, my loving friends.

Thought for the Day

Love is an action word.
Let's get busy!

September 28

Prayer for the Day

Father, we know who the author of confusion is—Satan. This tricky serpent knows just when and where to strike and seems to always do so in the midst of peace and serenity. We must stay on guard and never forget that we belong to you, and all good things come from you. Unless we stay close to you, Father, we will begin to have doubts that will be far from where you'd have us be. All things that are from the Father work out just how he planned them for our good and not to cause us harm.

My prayer for today is that God's children will resist the evil one and recognize all the tactics and flaming darts that Satan throws at us. That serpent is slick, but we shall draw nigh unto our God, and he will draw nigh unto us.

Amen and thank you, Lord.

Thought for the Day

He knew we would make mistakes. He figured that in when he handcrafted us! It's Friday! Rock it!

September 29

Prayer for the Day

Father, it is a beautiful day to be alive and how thankful I am for all things that are gifts from you. We grumble, but I don't know why. Maybe it's just our nature. Instead, I just want to always remember how you loved me so much that you saved me from myself and not only saved me but had the most wonderful way you wanted to use me. How beautiful is that?

My prayer for today is that we enjoy each day of our life and live at peace with all others and love, really love.

Amen and thank you, Lord.

Thought for the Day

Your mess that is now a message is one that is worth sharing. Psst, don't keep it a secret. It's good stuff!

September 30

Prayer for the Day

Father, here we are at the dawning of a new day. Did we wake with burdens? I pray not. Did we wake with a glad heart that embraces our hope and faith in you? I pray we did. Daily I am even more encouraged with my salvation, and although I am a person that is with flaws, I am not discouraged rather I am encouraged. You are with me until the end. You handpicked me and equipped me, so able to be a foot solider for your kingdom and your glory! I'm going to shout the house down this morning with my brothers and sisters, and we will sing and make music to you our precious Lord!

My prayer for today is that we never feel unworthy of God's love. He loves us unconditionally, and he said he would *never* leave us *nor* forsake us. That should give us all a reason to shout!

Amen and thank you, Lord.

Thought for the Day

There is always the sky and always enough space to fold two hands together.

October 1

Prayer for the Day

Father, we know that seven is the number of completion, and in Revelation 7:17, it says that God will wipe away every tear from their eyes. Take heart, weary soldiers; your efforts are not in vain. You will one day after a while be in our heavenly home with the Father, but until that time comes, fall in love with the Lord again. Make him your priority and remember that he is a jealous but just God, and if you love anything or anyone more than you love him, you are committing idolatry. Innocently, I know. Remember when you first found him and loved him. Be that way again, and he will be well pleased.

My prayer for today is that we walk by faith and not by sight, remembering always that the victory has already been claimed.

I pray that blessings of peace and hope will flood your heart today, and you shall be called victorious!

Amen and thank you, Lord.

Thought for the Day

The tribe of Judah shall come forth with a war cry that will shake the heavens, and we shall be victorious!

October 2

Prayer for the Day

Father, hallowed be thy name! I am praying for this world and praying for your people. Have you ever wondered why God hasn't already finished what he began? Because he wants none to perish. I am not at all trying to scare you, nor would I have you fearful, but there will be a day of reckoning for all of us. Our God loves us all, and he is no respecter of persons, so don't let guilt and shame hold you back from receiving what is rightfully yours!

My prayer for today is that we run to God and not from him. May we fall deeply and madly in love with him.

Amen and thank you, Lord.

Thought for the Day

God isn't mad at you. He's mad *about you!* How wonderful is that?

October 3

Prayer for the Day

Father, just like a brand-new day, we can be brand-new people. Rise up sleepers and take authority over your burdens, problems, and obstacles! We've had victories! Let's remember them and take heart.

My prayer for today is no matter the size of your problem, you never forget the size of our God.

Amen and thank you, Lord.

Thought for the Day

Remember your roots.
That's where you were planted.

October 4

Prayer for the Day

Father, good morning from the ones you love! Thank you for establishing a covenant with us and making sure that we would be able and equipped to withstand the dark forces of this world, but we don't want to dwell on the darkness, instead dwelling on the light and goodness of our Lord and Savior. Don't let what you see in the natural world throw you off balance, living with one foot in and one foot out! Stand firmly on the Word of God, and do not be carnally minded. Walk by faith, brothers and sisters, and pray. Always pray.

My prayer for today is that we take our rightful place as heirs to the kingdom and use the power God has supplied us with to make this world a better place.

Amen and thank you, Lord.

Thought for the Day

Days go slow, and years go fast. Use your time wisely, my friend. Love ya!

October 5

Prayer for the Day

Father, we know that we can't center our attention on what we see in the natural- and physical-sense realm. Everything is subject to change, so instead we shall put our faith in the unseen eternal realm. Remember that joy is not dependent on your circumstances. Do not judge a day as devoid of joy because it contains difficulties. Instead, concentrate on staying in touch with the Father.

My prayer for today is that we shall remember that your Word contains over seven thousand promises to cover any situation we will ever face, and no matter what happens in this shifting, changing world we live in, those promises will forever be the same.

Amen and thank you, Lord.

Thought for the Day

No two days are the same, but at the end of the day, he is still the same.
PS. It's Friday, and we're all still in one piece. Enjoy your weekend. Peace and love, friends.

October 6

Prayer for the Day

Father, we know that love never fails. Nothing works without it, and there can be no failure with it. When you live by love, you cannot fail. Agape love is a new kind of power. It makes you master of every situation. No weapon formed against you will prosper. No one even has the power to hurt your feelings because you are not ruled by feelings but by God's love. You are loving as he loves.

My prayer for today is that we are not overcome by evil but overcome evil with good, and if it is possible as far as it depends on you, live at peace with everyone.

Amen and thank you, Lord.

Thought for the Day

For love is truly the only sure secret to our success.

October 7

Prayer for the Day

Father, we stand at the dawning of a new day, and so we are blessed. I read through past posts, and I see where I have changed yet still the same. God took my rough places, and he smoothed me around the edges. He shaped my heart and mind to be Christlike, yet I still have a long road to travel, but, friends, I won't have to travel it alone. He will be with me, prompting me, guiding me, and always loving me. We don't have to look far for our help. Is he your best friend, and do you know that you can always say the name of Jesus, and there he will be?

My prayer for today is that we make the kingdom our first priority, and when we do all else, it will be added unto us.

Amen and thank you, Lord.

Thought for the Day

Amazing grace, it covers us all.
Have a beautiful Son Day. Get your praise and
worship on. It's good for your soul. Love ya!

October 8

Prayer for the Day

Father, we know you have given to all the same measure of faith and that our faith can be the size of a mustard seed, although I do pray that we have much more faith than that. A mustard seed is the smallest seed there is. My point is that if you have faith, no matter how small, you have the power to move mountains and speak to the trials you're facing, and in doing so, you have gained power. Don't let anything or anyone, especially your mountain(s), intimidate you. Take control again and watch your world begin to change for the better.

My prayer for today is that no matter what it looks like in the natural that we understand that we operate in the supernatural using all our gifts from our Lord and Savior to change not only our circumstances but the world in which we live.

Amen and thank you, Lord.

Thought for the Day

Just because and even though it's Monday, shine. I mean, really shine.

October 9

Prayer for the Day

Father, we know the cross will never be emptied of its power. We also know that you chose the foolish things of the world to shame the wise and that you chose the weak things of the world to shame the strong. God, you chose the lowly things of this world and the despised things and the things that are not to nullify the things that are so that no one may boast before you. What I'm trying to say is that we can never guess on what God is or will do. His thoughts and ways are so much higher than ours, and we limit what we think God will do. I dare you. Pray big; dream big. We've got a big God.

My prayer for today is that we take our rightful place once and for all as joint heirs to a kingdom that has already come.

Amen and thank you, Lord.

Thought for the Day

Make your life count!

October 10

Prayer for the Day

Father, we know that it is possible to live in this dangerous and unpredictable world because protection is a solid promise from you. Let me be clear, my brothers and sisters. God's promise of protection does not guarantee that the devil will leave you alone, but it does mean that God will give you an escape every time the devil rears its ugly head at you. This promise is for those that abide in the Word, staying in constant contact with the Lord and being in continual union with him. Those who live in the shadow of the Almighty possess the strength to overcome the evil one.

My prayer for today is that we remain connected to the only true and living God without fear or hesitation, knowing always that in him we place our hope.

Amen and thank you, Lord.

Thought for the Day

His love light never dims. Bask in the glow!

October 11

Prayer for the Day

Father, I believe we are living in the last days simply because of how much evil is going on around us, but this doesn't frighten me. It makes me cling to you even tighter, knowing that my faith will see me through the tough times, the times I am being persecuted or any other times. Walking with the Father gives us strength when we are weak, and we must stay prepared at all times since we know not when the hour will be. Are we ready, and are we building up the church and God's people? We all could do a little better. I'm sure, so we do not stumble when the load becomes heavy.

My prayer for today is that we build one another up in Christ Jesus and let the light that is in us shine like a beacon to our brothers and sisters who are lost and trying to find their way home.

Amen and thank you, Lord.

Thought for the Day

As for me and my home, we will serve the Lord.

October 12

Prayer for the Day

Father, even in the fiercest of temptations, we know right from wrong, yet we yield to temptations. We are not infallible just because we are God's people. We are humans that make mistakes. Proverbs tells us that pride goes before destruction, a haughty spirit before a fall. Paul taught in 1 Corinthians that God is faithful, and he will not put on us more than we can bear. Isn't that a relief to know that he knew we would make mistakes, yet he loves us anyway?

My prayer for today is that no matter what we think about or of ourselves that we really put on the mind-set of God and forgive ourselves and others.

Amen and thank you, Lord.

Thought for the Day

My conscience is clear, but that does not make me innocent. Refer to 1 Corinthians 44.

October 13

Prayer for the Day

Father, good morning, and thank you, Lord, for giving me breath in my body. My back is strong and my mind sharp. These days of late have been so peaceful and filled with days of contentment. Time spent with my son has been full of quality mom-and-son time, and I have looked around and seen the beauty in everything. There has been a lazy contentment surrounding me, and I am enjoying life as you would have me to. I feel power when I read and study your Word, and I pray and believe when I do. I claim victory and not defeat in all of my burdens, and I am not chained but loosed with the power of your spirit.

My prayer for today is that as your children, we never forget our worth and value, sending your only Son to die a criminal's death so that forevermore we would walk in the light instead of the dark! Hallelujah and praise be to the Father!

Amen and thank you, Lord.

Thought for the Day

It's a great day to be alive. Live your days and enjoy the moments.

October 14

Prayer for the Day

Father, you have loved your children through the ages, and you have kept your promises through thick and thin. Now it is up to us to be the people you called us to be. This call isn't about perfection, but it is about focusing our lives on God and not on ourselves. Overcoming selfishness starts with turning our focus away from ourselves and onto God. We have God's power, love, and strength as we seek to build lives that glorify him.

My prayer for today is that we build one another up in love and model our life to be a reflection of the true and living God that we serve.

Amen and thank you, Lord.

Thought for the Day

When you build up others, you gain strength to face your own battles. Praying you have a peaceful and blessed Son Day.

October 15

Prayer for the Day

Father, from whom all blessings flow, thank you for another sunrise. Another day has been given that was not promised. Forgive others, love hard, and always give thanks to our Father that loves us so much. Yes, life is but a vapor, but before the vapor was and is, there is life, and he wants us to live it to the fullest.

My prayer for today is that we all remain rooted in our precious Lord, knowing that if he is for us—and he is—nothing can come against us.

Amen and thank you, Lord.

Thought for the Day

God bless your day, and praise God.
Be a blessing to somebody else!

October 16

Prayer for the Day

Father, my heart is so full right now. Multiple things happened in my life that gave me confirmation in my spirit that you never take your eyes off of your children. Patience is key when we pray. We may have a distorted view of patience, believing it is designed to help us suffer failure gracefully. According to the scriptures, patience will actually put us on the path to success. Patience is the power twin of faith. If we base our confidence on the Word of God, we will see that it says the same thing yesterday that it will today.

My prayer for today is that we allow our faith to open doors to God's promise for each of us according to our needs. I pray that we can put patience to work, knowing that the Word guarantees you will receive what you need.

Amen and thank you, Lord.

Thought for the Day

A closed mouth will not get fed.
Open up and tell our mighty God what you need.
Yes, he already knows, but he's waiting
for you to ask in his Son's name.

October 17

Prayer for the Day

Father, I have been blessed. I have done things and been to places that I never imagined because I refused to stay where I was, and you refused to leave me there. It makes me want to cry tears of joy. I know the Lord has a good purpose for each of us, and if you'll spend time with him, he will reveal the way in which he would have you walk. I have lived longer than I have left to live, but I'm going to make each day count.

My prayer for the day is that no matter what it looks like in the natural, you will begin to operate in the supernatural, calling life and not death into all your burdens. I pray this practice of operating in the supernatural will come as easily as drawing our next breath.

Amen and thank you, Lord.

Thought for the Day

I wouldn't take nothing for my journey now.
Psst. Hey, you, yeah you, I love you.
Now walk it out. Walk it out.

October 18

Prayer for the Day

Father, we can see beauty everywhere we look, or we can grumble about everything we see. I choose to be peculiar, called out in fact as one of God's chosen people, believing there is a purpose for each of us. No matter what we're going through, there is a purpose for your pain. It is not necessary to understand what God is doing, but it is necessary that you trust him. He takes us through the fire to refine us for his glory. With that, I can live with.

My prayer for today is that we stand on the rock of faith, believing with all we have that God is working all things out for our good.

Amen and thank you, Lord.

Thought for the Day

With him all things are possible.

October 19

Prayer for the Day

Father, just as we know a house divided against itself will fall, also if we come together in the unity of our faith, we'll arrive at the full stature of Christ Jesus and him glorified! Speaking truth and love grows you up while fuss and envy separates us and returns us to *babyhood*. Refuse to let Satan hinder your spiritual growth.

My prayer for today is that we learn to speak the language of love and grow up into him in all things.

Amen and thank you, Lord.

Thought for the Day

If we keep taking one step forward and three steps back, we have accomplished exactly nothing. In fact, we are farther back than when we first began.

October 20

Prayer for the Day

Father, sometimes I feel like we think we're *stuck* on earth, waiting to get to heaven just so all our troubles will be over. Instead, we need to realize that the things we face on earth are meant to grow us, to increase our faith, and to bring glory to the name that is above all other names. We can live a good life here on earth, but to do so, we must let go of the life we are accustomed to, instead setting our hearts on what you want us to do. We must be like Jesus. He lived his life to please the Father. He did only what the Father told him to do, and he lived in total victory.

My prayer for today is that we lay down our lives in order to fulfill his desires, realizing that our purpose is to please God.

Amen and thank you, Lord, (Mark 8:34–35).

Thought for the Day

It's time to realize that getting born again is not something we do in order just to miss hell.

October 21

Prayer for the Day

Father, sometimes I don't think we realize how truly blessed we are. It's tough to believe yourself *rich* when all your bills are due or an emergency financial crisis pops up, but we are in a covenant of prosperity with you, and you will prosper us! It is not wrong to want to prosper because our prosperity allows us to bless others. The purpose of God establishing us in prosperity is so that we may give to others in need. Never give grudgingly when you give in the name of the Lord. Instead, give with joy and expect nothing in return.

My prayer for today is that we give according to our heart as opposed to what we think we have. Father, I pray that we snap out of this mental state of poverty and despair and start believing you for all our needs!

Amen and thank you, Lord.

Thought for the Day

We cannot outgive God. He has a storehouse of blessings that he's just waiting to pour out on you!

October 22

Prayer for the Day

Father, just as we know good works won't save us, we know it is the receiving of the faith, the inclining of the ear, the profession of the heart that receives Jesus as Lord! We can toil and tarry all day, but when you receive a touch from a true and living God, it puts a pep to your step. It lifts sagging arms that will praise you holy. He's able. Our God is able to do far above what you think is possible. Take the limits off God and watch him do a good work in your life, watch your dreams come to fruition. I double dog dare you to dream big! After all, he's a big God.

My prayer for today is that we return to the simple yet true worship and praise that gets our God's attention. Oh, he's a jealous God, so I pray that you don't divide your worship and sacrifice to anyone or anything else but him.

Amen and thank you, Lord.

Thought for the Day

Arise, sleepers! It's time to get it. We got this. Even though and just because it's Monday, we got this 'cause he's got us.

October 23

Prayer for the Day

Father, my praise belongs to you as I stand at the dawning of a new day with endless possibilities. I feel strong and able to tackle anything that comes my way. This feeling didn't just happen. It took hard work and dedication to arrive at this destination. Thank you, Lord, that I am not where I used to be, but I am not yet where I am going.

My prayer for today is that we stand firm in our convictions to not allow anything to disrupt our course we've been chosen to follow.

Amen and thank you, Lord.

Thought for the Day

In him we cannot fail.

October 24

Prayer for the Day

Father, when a man is drowning and a life jacket is thrown to him, he grabs it! And so it is with the Word; it is a life jacket to navigate the course of life. God puts people in your path, and there are no mistakes in his plan. Don't be too proud to ask for help or say, "I need help." There are people that care enough to help you and allow your light to shine for Jesus because our light is shining.

My prayer for today is that we as Christians never get on the *high horse*, forgetting where we came from and by all means not forgetting where we are going! Don't ask for a blessing today; instead, be the blessing!

Amen and thank you, Lord.

Thought for the Day

When you are thankful, you are eager
to give of yourself. Who needs me today?
I'm here. I'm right here.

October 25

Prayer for the Day

Father, we take so much for granted, like waking up and having the strength to move across the floor with ease. Nothing is by chance in life. You can rub all the rabbit's feet in the world, but you can't assure yourself anything. We are not in an accidental position in life; rather we are exactly where he wants us to be. He moves me. I make mistakes and move on my own sometimes, and it doesn't work out, but when God moves you into position, expect great things to happen. If we can remember that his ways are so much higher than ours, then we can learn to wait for him to move.

My prayer for today is that we can adjust our stride to the rhythm of life like ebb and flow. Don't be too impatient, for when we do, we are setting ourselves up for failure. Wait patiently for the Lord. I say wait.

Amen and thank you, Lord.

Thought for the Day

He knows my name, every move that I make. Yes, he knows my name.

October 26

Prayer for the Day

Father, everyone's perception of reality is different, and it makes it neither right nor wrong, but what they see as truth is what they stand by. I know that you are truth, Lord, and in you, truth will always prevail. Seek the truth while it may still be found. Seek the Lord. We live in a world that gives subliminal messages, and we are constantly bombarded with hidden meanings. We walk as children of the light, and our lamps are lit and burn brightly.

My prayer for today is that we assume our rightful place beside Jesus. After all, that was God's purpose for Calvary—to bring us alongside Jesus.

Amen and thank you, Lord.

Thought for the Day

You and I are the reason Jesus came to earth and died and lived again. This gives us the right to wear his name and wield his authority on earth.

October 27

Prayer for the Day

Father, our cup surely runneth over. If we can fix our hearts and minds on what we have and not be envious of what others have, then we can say we are indeed blessed. Are you fearful that there is a shortage of abounding grace? (Enough to go around.) Checking Romans 5:20, it says, "The more we see our sinfulness, the more we see God's abounding grace forgiving us." I count my blessings when I get down in the dumps, and in doing so, I find myself less likely to grumble. How about you? Are you blessed? Does your cup runneth over? Does his grace overcome our sin? Yes, yes, and yes!

My prayer for today is that we will pray and thank God for what we have, counting the very blessing of being alive first.

Amen and thank you, Lord!

Thought for the Day

We are blessed people.

October 28

Prayer for the Day

Father, our meditation was right on time this morning. In regard to being treated fairly in life, do not expect this to happen. In fact, it is my belief that the closer we walk with you, the harder the devil works to undermine our path. If we can recognize these *growing pains* and walk in them gracefully, we will never have to regret these times or possibly these people. If you know in your heart that your intentions are pure, walk on. Work faithfully on what the Lord has set before you, and just because and even though you may encounter obstacles, count them as pure joy, for you won't be the same as you walk in grace.

My prayer for today is that we will consult with you, Lord and not set out on our own praying always for your watchful eye to guard us and lead us.

Amen and thank you, Lord.

Thought for the Day

Because of who I am, in him all things are possible. Prayers for a peaceful and blessed Son Day for each of you.

October 29

Prayer for the Day

Father, good morning from your loved ones. Some grumble because it's Monday. I say, don't grumble. Be thankful! How many didn't wake to see this beautiful sunrise? It's not a perfect life we're living, but by staying with eyes fixed on truth, we can make it! I believe we are growing in strength when we do life without complaining as much. After all, it seems easier to be happy than unhappy, but don't you have people in your life that if you ask them how they are, they're sure to tell you how they are? So many complaints. Life is truly a gift, and personally, I know the best is yet to come.

My prayer for today is that we consider all we have and focus on the positive aspects of life and give to God that which tries to weigh us down.

Amen and thank you, Lord.

Thought for the Day

Don't let anything or anyone steal your shine.

October 30

Prayer for the Day

Father, David was a shepherd that tended sheep. No matter how many sheep he had, if even one wandered off or was hurt, that was where David's attention was. The Bible makes mention of the sheep. If there are ninety-nine and even one wanders off, put a little perspective on this, and remember that no matter what we do, don't do, have done, or will ever do, Jesus loves us. When we begin to realize that our lives and every aspect of our lives matter to him, then we can begin to draw close, real close, closer than a brother. Heaven is what awaits the believer. Yes, and that's wonderful, but how about today? Can we live each day with joy, unspeakable joy because of a man named Jesus? Yes, yes, we can!

My prayer for today is that we change our thinking about Jesus, and we stop waiting for him to come realizing that he is already here! Makes me want to start shouting!

Amen and thank you, Lord!

Thought for the Day

Cattle are herded. Sheep are tended.
Aww, he tends to me. How beautiful is that?

October 31

Prayer for the Day

Father, I'm watching Ryder sleep, and he's crawled all over our king-size bed and awakened several times during the night, but I was right there, attentive to what this fourteen-month-old baby was doing. Now imagine yourself to be a *baby*. The Lord our God never takes his eyes off his children. I slept and slumbered. The scripture says, "He who never rests nor slumbers." He is always, and I mean, always watching over us. That's reassuring to me. How about you? Are you confident about life and relaxing in his arms? If not, I want you to try confidence on like a new coat.

My prayer for today is that as children of the Most High God, we are not fearful but prayerful about the things in life that cause us concern. When you practice faith instead of fear, you'll soon be walking in victory!

Amen and thank you, Lord.

Thought for the Day

For Halloween, let's really be Christians instead of just dressing up like Christians for Sunday service. It begins in the heart—change.

November 1

Prayer for the Day

Father, lugging a baby around all day is hard work. Although we are thankful, we weren't prepared. If we had been prepared, we would have had something to sit him in. And that's how life is. If you aren't prepared, things can knock you off your feet. You can never meditate enough, pray enough, or love God too much because each day his mercies are new, and we have something to thank him for all over again. I don't know about you, but God has been good to me and my family. He's blessed us and loved us through the good and the not so good.

Through it all, we're still standing, and we're still shouting about a man named Jesus.

My prayer for today is that we line ourselves up in God's will and allow him to love us and teach us to love ourselves.

Amen and thank you, Lord.

Thought for the Day

Are you walking in the will of God?

November 2

Prayer for the Day

Father, when we put things into perspective, it seems much easier to understand. We know Jesus was born of a woman. He was the Godhead and not God. We know he was tempted by every sin known to man, yet he did not sin. So this is where we go with what we know. Jesus gave us, you and me, the power of the Holy Spirit and anointed us, you and me, to take charge of our burdens, overcome the evil one, or perhaps lay hands on the sick. Don't let this power scare you or go to your head. Pray for him to operate in you and walk in line with the Father.

My prayer today is that we as children of the light will take our rightful place and begin to operate out of the very power that flows from him to us.

Amen and thank you, Lord.

Thought for the Day

Stay connected to him and you'll never lose power.

November 3

Prayer for the Day

Father, there are so many advantages to having a large family! It used to be about normal to raise a family of nine or so. Now the average family has around two. I always thought I would like to be a part of a large family. Praise God for answering my prayers! I am a part of the family of Christ, and I have so many brothers and sisters. I can't even count them all! Now don't get me wrong. My family isn't perfect, but the last time I checked, we weren't supposed to be. We simply walk in love, praying for others and allowing God to use us to spread the good news of the gospel.

My prayer for today is that if you feel alone or know loneliness, I pray that you will reach out and find out about all your other brothers and sisters.

Amen and thank you, Lord.

Thought for the Day

No DNA necessary. He is our Father!

November 4

Prayer for the Day

Father, it's been a busy week. We've had the baby and events to attend. I have pondered all week at how this baby is mostly satisfied with anything. Life delights him. We should be more like the baby in that regard. Another thing I've marveled at is how there is almost always something going on in Rome. We've got people in our town with a hunger to help people, and I have been moved by the kindness of absolute strangers. Yes, it's easy to grumble, but if we look around, there is something to always be thankful for. Only one percent of our world is on drugs, and ninety-nine percent are living normal lives. That surprised me years ago when I was in my addiction because I thought everybody was on drugs, but I thought of that because that's the only people I saw. I am satisfied now to be in the other part, the ninety-nine percent part. When you change the way you think, the way you think will change.

My prayer for today is that we will begin to humble ourselves before God and help his people. He didn't bless us so we could sit on our testimony and keep it a secret. He blesses us so that we can bless others, and I pray that today we do.

Amen and thank you, Lord.

Thought for the Day

No two days are the same, yet he always is. May the Son shine his light on your life today so that you will be able to help others shine.

November 5

Prayer for the Day

Father, I get my feelings hurt real easy, but I'm working on that. I realize that when people do hurt me or I feel slighted in some way, Satan was involved. We forget that he is our enemy and blame our friends instead. Doesn't the Bible tell us that we wrestle not with flesh and blood, so people cannot be the source of our problem? It must be something else. Instead of being hurt or mad, try praying for these people and those situations. You'll soon be delighted with the outcome. Besides, fighting and fussing is not our style.

My prayer for today is that we take authority over our problems in the name of Jesus, and, Lord, let us not be operating in the enemy's name but your sweet name. Oh how we love you.

Amen and thank you, Lord.

Thought for the Day

God has the final word.

November 6

Prayer for the Day

Father, if we can take hold of the knowledge that we are winners not meant to live in defeat, then we surely can begin to shout the victory. I've got a lot of good going in my life right now. I refuse to be defeated by anything or anyone, especially the tactics of the enemy! Adopt this mind-set, brothers and sisters. I can't tell you your trials won't come. I can't tell you that testing won't come. I can't tell you hard times won't hit, but what I can tell you is that we have the one that is able to help us through these things and come out a winner! His name is Jesus, and the truth will stand as the world crumbles. I feel led this morning to urge you to give it all up, lay it all down. I feel like someone needs an encouraging word that he will not leave you where you are! When you begin to see that whatever we go through is meant to grow us, then we can begin to view trials in a different light. My prayer for today is that we truly lay it down. I pray that you will allow our Lord and Savior to be the name that slips off your tongue when you need help.

Amen and thank you, Lord.

Thought for the Day

We are blessed going in and blessed coming out, so that just about tells me to get somewhere! Have a beautiful day!

November 7

Prayer for the Day

Father, you instilled in me a survivor's mentality. You gave me a strength to dig out when I dug myself in. I could sit around today having a pity party, or I can work with what I have and change the outcome. I choose the latter. And so it is with everyone. We will face obstacles, but we cannot throw in the towel. We have to stand flat footed and work with what we have to get to where we're going!

My prayer for today is that no matter what we are facing, we recognize that it is not as big as the God we serve. I pray, Father, for all of us to recognize that we are not helpless, and the situation is not hopeless.

Amen and thank you, Lord.

Thought for the Day

He is our ever present help.

November 8

Prayers for the Day

Father, here we are in all our humaneness, needing you again. No other love is like your love. Other love keeps score, mistreats, knocks you down, not your love. This love sends us off on our day with a confidence that no matter what we're able, I like to feel confident and not confused. It just seems like you're not getting anywhere when you're confused. God looks at us with compassion and mercy, and he is not unaware of what we need, although he does require that we ask.

That's pretty reassuring.

My prayer for today is that we are confident in our Christian walk, having the confidence that no matter what we face, he's already there.

Amen and thank you, Lord.

Thought for the Day

*Do not despise small beginnings.
You don't know what he has in mind.*

November 9

Prayer for the Day

Father, this is the day that you have made, and I will rejoice and be glad in it. Bible. Feelings point you in another direction sometimes, don't they? It seems as if the world is stacked against you; the wind blows in your face instead of at your back. No feeling is final, and emotions are not a true gauge of your situation. When we begin to grasp the thought that Jesus loves us and we are not alone, we can begin to gain strength and view things differently. Each day we are alive means we have hope that a dream will come true; a prayer will be answered.

My prayer for today is that we never stop working on achieving what the desires of our heart are. The Lord said that he would give them to us. I pray you rest on this promise.

Amen and thank you, Lord.

Thought for the Day

Never, never give up. Giving up is not an option.

November 10

Prayer for the Day

Father, I have been strengthened by the many people I know who have turned their hearts and lives over to you. Some are big, strong men that quote scripture and talk about Jesus. I don't consider that to be unmanly at all. The most beautiful women I know talk about grace and forgiveness. I'm not envious of their beauty. These same people that can tell you about Jesus also can tell you how it used to be. Our lives used to be a mess, and yes, some were on drugs; some weren't.

People don't have to be on drugs for their life to be a mess. Without the heavenly Father to guide us, we'll all drift aimlessly. I like knowing that no matter what I'm facing, he's there to help me along. Don't you? He's a way maker, a pain taker.

Only he can give the freedom you're looking for, and if you just lay it all down, he will hold you up with his righteousness.

My prayer for today is that you realize that you have value and worth. There's something that you're longing to accomplish, and I pray that you ask God to help you with all your dreams. They're closer than you think.

Amen and thank you, Lord.

Thought for the Day

If getting to know the Father is on your bucket list, why not begin today? There's no time like the present.

November 11

Prayer for the Day

Father, if I lost it all today, I'd still have you. You don't change like the shifting shadows, and you aren't going to change your mind about loving me. That love is eternal and secure. Whew, that means he loves me regardless, and I can rest on it.
Amen and thank you, Lord.

Thought for the Day

The mind is a battlefield. What do you think it takes to be victorious?

November 12

Prayer for the Day

Father, good morning, and bless your holy name! I feel excited this morning, and the rain doesn't bother me, and nothing else is going to bother me. I feel absolutely energized after church yesterday and the singing. Lord, we had it going good, but that was yesterday, and we can have that same feeling today. Pastor says we can have a throne-room experience. How do we do this? We believe him for everything we need in our life and remember that God wants to bless us! I'll take a blessing. Will you?

My prayer for today is that we all stop thinking God is out to get us and believe him for our blessings. I pray that whatever you need that our God who supplied all your riches will be exalted before all man. Whew! Now that is something to get excited about!

Amen and thank you, Lord.

Thought for the Day

Rainy days and Mondays do not get me down!

November 13

Prayer for the Day

Heavenly Father, another day has been given, and I thank you. I pray that all this hate, violence, and protesting will stop. As you look down, you don't get worried the way I do because you know what we're going to do before we do. We don't surprise you. I will try and worry less and pray harder after all. I know how things are going to turn out in the end. You're a good, good Father, and I'm thankful that you took time to help me straighten out my life. Now can we work on my temper?

Amen and thank you, Lord.

Thought for the Day

What's love got to do with it? Everything.

November 14

Prayer for the Day

Father, I've seen good times, and I've been through some bad. How sweet it is coming out of the valley, knowing you were praising him, confident that he never moved. My prayer for today is this that I'll never give up. I am strong enough every day to be the victor and not the victim.

Amen and thank you, Lord.

Thought for the Day

Worthy is the Lamb.

November 15

Prayer for the Day

Father, I wake up, and I'm feeling safe because I know you watched over me as I slept last night. I look out the window and see the beauty you created for us to enjoy. I have an inner peace that will stay with me throughout my day, and I won't worry about things that I have no control over. My prayer for today is that we will all begin to relax and lean into your arms, embracing life as you give it to us.

Amen and thank you, Lord.

Thought for the Day

Remember, we are blessed going in and blessed coming out. He is the maker and the breaker, the giver and the taker. He will see you through.

November 16

Prayer for the Day

Father, so many times I moved before you said move. Too many times I got in your way and wouldn't allow you to do your work. I was impatient and too aggressive. I have been hearing from you, and oh, how I praised you when the wisdom came. Today, Lord, I pray that I will continue my voyage with my ears open and waiting for that small still voice to be my helper.

Amen and thank you, Lord.

Thought for the Day

Be patient as you wait for the Lord.

November 17

Prayer for the Day

Father, I look around, and I am constantly surprised at the strength I have found in you. All times can't be nor will be perfect, but it's at those times of life's imperfectness that you are so perfect. Little things mean so much to me, and I'm thankful for your presence in my life.

Amen and thank you, Lord.

Thought for the Day

Little is much when God is in it.

November 18

Prayer for the Day

Father, when we are having problems, we try the easiest route to alleviate the pain. We shouldn't, for they are teaching tools. Really they are just uncomfortable situations, and these are the times when and if we will allow you, you do magnificent work. I am handcrafted by the potter; therefore, I know he made me just the way he intended for me to be. When you are in an *uncomfortable situation*, think on those things that are lovely and good. My prayer is that I count my blessings before I grumble.

Amen and thank you, Lord.

Thought for the Day

We gonna keep slugging at it!

November 19

Prayer for the Day

Father, money can't buy happiness. Nothing can buy joy. The things of this world are fleeting and will fade away, but we know our treasures are stored up in heaven. How lonesome I would be without you. It's so comforting to know when I need you, there you are Lord. I pray that I always do my part to bring your kingdom to the hurting souls I see daily.

Amen and thank you, Lord.

Thought for the Day

If we do our part, he will surely do his.

November 20

Prayer for the Day

Father, life is fleeting, a vapor in fact. Be kind to people; you don't know what they're going through. A smile, a visit, a kind word may make such a difference. I pray, Lord, to never forget that I am made in your image and that love is the core of my foundation. Praying that we all can share love like it's the most important thing in the world because it is.

Amen and thank you, Lord.

Thought for the Day

I don't know what tomorrow holds, but I do know who holds tomorrow.

November 21

Prayer for the Day

Father, we must admit our helplessness before our prayer for help will be heard by you. Our own need must be recognized before we can ask you for strength to meet that need. Once that need is recognized, our prayers are heard above all the music of heaven. Lord, we pray that we may send our voiceless cry for help out into that void. We pray that we may feel certain that it will be heard somewhere somehow.

Amen and thank you, Lord.

Thought for the Day

It is not theological arguments that solve the problems of the questioning soul but the sincere cry of the soul to God for strength and the certainty of that soul that the cry will be heard and answered.

November 22

Prayer for the Day

Father, my praise is music to your ears. The hardest concept I ever learned to grasp was praising you through the valleys. When you got to the mountain, it made it so much sweeter. There will always be troubles among us, but I pray God that we always remember and never forget that you are with us. We are stronger than we know because of the strength you give us.

Amen and thank you, Lord.

Thought for the Day

Ain't no bird going to sing in my place; as long as I'm alive, I'll testify.

November 23

Prayer for the Day

Father, Thanksgiving isn't where or what you eat; it's about what's in your heart. My prayer today is that all the world can feel thankful that we are free in a land that provides so many liberties. I do pray, Lord, for there to be love and peace today and every day. Amen and thank you, Lord.

Thought for the Day

Spread peace and love today the way you're spreading butter on those rolls. Happy Thanksgiving. Gobble till you wobble.

November 24

Prayer for the Day

Father, I am thankful for all your blessings, especially because you didn't leave me where I was. I pray for your strength today, and I won't try to rely on my own. My heart is full today yet very heavy as we say goodbye to my uncle Steve. My prayer for today is that I will rest against you and draw wisdom and courage from you.
    Amen and thank you, Lord.

Thought for the Day

Accept and love people for who they are. It's not our place to judge them, but it is our duty to love them.

November 25

Prayer for the Day

Heavenly Father, thank you for another day. I pray, Lord, for those that are stumbling around unsure of themselves and feeling they are battling life by themselves. There is a God, and he is real. I know because he saved me from a devil's hell. All times aren't perfect, and they're not supposed to be, but I do know where to get my help from, the Master himself.

Amen and thank you, Lord.

Thought for the Day

That one is God. May you find him now.

November 26

Prayer for the Day

Father, every day is a near-death experience since we are to die daily. Flesh wants what makes it happy and will not accept delayed gratification unless we surrender our hearts to you every single day. Father, I pray for your Spirit to indwell with my spirit and therefore be pleasing unto you.

Amen and thank you, Lord.

Thought for the Day

It is not by chance that you woke up this morning. God has plans for you.

November 27

Prayer for the Day

Father, thinking of how you have blessed me creates in me an even stronger desire to be humble. You took me as dirty, filthy rags and cleaned me up in the image of your glory. I will praise you, and I pray that I always remember that on my own I am nothing, and I can do nothing without you.
    Amen and thank you, Lord.

Thought for the Day

What he did for me, he'll do for you.

November 28

Prayer for the Day

Father, some of us may feel we don't have much to offer people in need. Our life may be in ruins; we may have gone into debt to support destructive habits. Even if we have nothing else to give, we can share our story of how God gave us a second chance. As little as this may seem to us, it may be the gift of life to someone in the throes of addiction. Father, I pray that I never pass up the opportunity to tell someone about you.
Amen and thank you, Lord.

Thought for the Day

The more spiritual seeds we plant by generously helping others, the greater will be our harvest of spiritual fruit.

November 29

Prayer for the Day

Self-control is not willpower. It is not gritting your teeth and forcing yourself to just say no. Self-control is called a fruit. Fruit doesn't instantly pop out on the tree. As the tree grows and seasons pass, the fruit naturally develops. As we continue to follow God's guidance, taking one step at a time, our self-control will gradually grow. Father, I pray we stay connected to you. We know it is the Holy Spirit's job to produce the fruit of self-control in our life.
 Amen and thank you, Lord.

Thought for the Day

But when the Holy Spirit controls our lives, he will produce this kind of fruit in us—love, joy, patience, peace, kindness, goodness, faithfulness, and self-control.

November 30

Prayer for the Day

Father, if we are not willing to trust and obey you, we soon become enslaved to other things. We turn to other activities or substances to help deal with our problems. Most of us realize that this often leads to various forms of addiction. We have discovered that drugs, alcohol, sexual immorality, work, or even religious activities can never solve our problems. In fact, depending on anything other than God himself leads to even deeper problems. My prayer is that there is a turning to God, not from him, so that we might be able to be productive and helpful to those around us.

Amen and thank you, Lord.

Thought for the Day

Only God offers us the power to be delivered from bondage to build a new life. Turning to him for help is really the only valid option we have.

December 1

Prayer for the Day

Father, a new day has come for us, and the possibilities are endless. Thank you, Lord, for not leaving us where we were, and thank you, Lord, that you're not finished with us yet.
Amen and thank you, Lord.

Thought for the Day

One nation under God.

December 2

Prayer for the Day

Father, only you can bring comfort to our broken hearts. We don't utilize the gifts you have given us. We have power in our bodies to do so much, yet we let it lie stale and dormant. I pray that all believers will start pulling down the strongholds of addiction in our community. It's going to take all of us, but change will come if we exercise our faith.

Amen and thank you, Lord.

Thought for the Day

Use the talents God gifted you with to change what may seem unchangeable.

December 3

Prayer for the Day

Father, in times of trouble, we often search for the thunder and lightning of your voice and direction. Mistakenly, we think that you will provide us with the solutions we seek in some spectacular way. The truth of the matter is that the answers lie within us.

Amen and thank you, Lord.

Thought for the Day

Only step by step, stage by stage, can we proceed in our journey into greater knowledge and understanding.

December 4

Prayer for the Day

Father, thank you for the dawning of a new day. I feel hopeful about my life and the people I love, not helpless. If these four walls crumbled down on me, I would be telling you how much I love you. You have never failed me, and I know you never will.
   Amen and thank you, Lord.

Thought for the Day

*I've changed, yet I'm still the same.
My missing ingredient was a
relationship with God.*

December 5

Prayer for the Day

Father, we pray to give something to those whose thoughts are confused, something to those having troubles, something of our sympathy, our prayers, our time, our love, ourselves. I pray we give of our own confidence as we have had it given to us by your grace. Give of yourself and your loving sympathy. Give your best to those who need it and will accept it. I pray, Father, that as I have received, so may I give. I pray that I may have the right answer to those who are confused. Amen and thank you, Lord.

Thought for the Day

Give according to need, never according to deserts. Remember that the giving of advice can never take the place of giving of yourself.

December 6

Prayer for the Day

Father, self-indulgence gets a lot of us in trouble. The pleasures offered by God should be enjoyed with thanksgiving. Deprivation leads to a deeper hunger, but God has given us so many earthly pleasures to enjoy. We should hunger for nothing. When we learn to replace our enslaving dependency with wholesome activities, we will be less tempted to escape life through addiction.

Amen and thank you, Lord.

Thought for the Day

We can make progress in recovery if we are willing to train hard and take the first steps.

December 7

Prayer for the Day

Father, for each person in my life, there is a reason. I am so thankful when I see people I haven't seen in a while. It warms my heart. To people I don't even know, I want to know you. Can I help you? Do you need something that I can provide?

You are precious in his sight, so you are precious in my sight. My heart is full of love, and I don't mind sharing anything I have, for God has provided for all my needs. I pray, Lord, to be that person that went the extra mile to help someone who needed me. I need them more than they'll ever need me.

Lord, keep me strong.

Amen and thank you, Lord.

Thought for the Day

I count my blessings, and in doing so, I find I really have nothing to grumble about.

December 8

Prayer for the Day

Father, recovery and spiritual growth are never easy. Progress requires that we follow the principles of disciplined faith on a daily basis. Like soldiers, we need to put aside the obstacles to our spiritual growth—our dependency, our pursuit of pleasure, our denial. Like farmers, we need to work hard, persevering through the tough times. If we follow these examples, God will work in our life and help us win life's hard battles. He will reward us with understanding and a rich harvest of blessings. Lord, I pray that we have hope only in you to face the battles in our life.

Amen and thank you, Lord.

Thought for the Day

The power of God is behind all good works.

December 9

Prayer for the Day

Father, I pray that my soul will lose its restlessness by finding rest in you. I pray that I may find peace of mind in the thought of you and your purpose for my life.
Amen and thank you, Lord.

Thought for the Day

We are all seeking something, but many do not know what they want in life. Our search will end when we find faith and trust in God for the answer.

December 10

Prayer for the Day

Father, thank you for waking me up this morning. You always do your part. I pray, Lord, to do mine.
    Amen and thank you, Lord.

Thought for the Day

Snow beauties, everything it covers.

December 11

Prayer for the Day

Father, most of us have a hard time modeling submission and humility, qualities that are essential for the recovery process because they show dependence on God and a willingness to be guided by him. Satan's pride and our adoption of it opposes God's program for healthy and godly living. As many of us know from experience, the way of pride and selfishness only leads to confusion and strife. My prayer is to throw away any pride I have in the things of this world and depend on him.

Thought for the Day

True contentment comes only when we submit our life to God, admitting our failures humbly seeking to do his will.

December 12

Prayer for the Day

Father, we know that love and fear cannot dwell together. By their very natures, they cannot exist side by side. A strong love, a love that trusts in God, is sure to eventually conquer fear. Father, how I pray that love will drive out the fear in my life, and I pray that my fear will flee before the power of the love of God.

Amen and thank you, Lord.

Thought for the Day

The only sure way to dispel fear is to have the love of God more and more in your heart and soul.

December 13

Prayer for the Day

Father, another day has come for us. Some of us know we are still here only by the grace of God. The mere fact that we are here says to me that there is much work left to do. I pray so sincerely to be better each day than the day before. All times will not be perfect, and those times are when I will find out how much strength I have.
    Amen and thank you, Lord.

Thought for the Day

    I will praise the Lord in all days that end in y.

December 14

Prayer for the Day

Father, as I began to pray to you, let me always start with praise and thanksgiving. I understand that my prayers are heard because I have a relationship with you, not because of anything I've done. I pray, God, to never forget where you brought me from and to always remember where I am going.

Amen and thank you, Lord.

Thought for the Day

Present your prayers to God with anticipation and trust his answers.

December 15

Prayer for the Day

Father, sometimes there seems to be a shadow on my life, and I feel out of sorts. I pray, God, to realize this is not the withdrawal of your presence in my life but my temporary unwillingness to realize it. I pray I may face the dull days with courage, praying in faith that the bright days will return.
    Amen and thank you, Lord.

Thought for the Day

The quiet, gray days are the days for doing what you must do, knowing that the presence of God's nearness will return and be with you when the gray days are past.

December 16

Prayer for the Day

Father, I have been through many seasons in my life. I've been on the mountain, and I've lain in the valley. I have used excuses to justify my wrong actions and hurt people I truly love. As this life keeps going, so shall I. I know right from wrong, and I believe that one day we will all answer for the life we have lived.

My prayer, Lord, is to remind myself daily that I am loved by you and that I can do all things through you that has strengthened me.

Amen and thank you, Lord.

Thought for the Day

Because he lives, I can face tomorrow.

December 17

Prayer for the Day

Father, when we are able to accept ourselves as imperfect people living in an imperfect world, then we can really begin the process of living each day to the fullest. Accepting people for who they are and loving them even when they don't live up to your expectations, that is genuine.

My prayer for today is that we stop hanging labels on people and just love them not because we have to but because we want to.

Amen and thank you, Lord.

Thought for the Day

Each one of us have love to give.
There's someone that needs to be loved.

December 18

Prayer for the Day

Father, I know now why people get depressed at Christmas. Loved ones gone, empty chairs, a house that once held laughter now holds only memories. Hold close the ones that love you and cherish each day as it comes.

My prayer for all of us is that the true meaning of Christmas settles in on our heart, and we don't give up just because life changed forever.

Amen and thank you, Lord.

Thought for the Day

Each day brings a hope to our heart that we know we can survive even the darkest hours.

December 19

Prayer for the Day

Father, I thank you for what I have experienced in life, even the times when I thought I would surely crumble and break. I didn't. I was made strong by events that I had no control over. Wasn't it then that you held me up and gave me the will to survive and by surviving help others survive? I often ask, "What is my purpose for still being here?" My purpose is your will, not mine.

My prayer for today is that we accept the will of God as being perfect, and no mistake was made when he moved however he moved. Amen and thank you, Lord.

Thought for the Day

All things work for the glory of God. He's perfect and does not require us to be anything but willing.

December 20

Prayer for the Day

Father, thank you that when I couldn't love myself, you did. Forgiveness of self is one of the hardest things I've ever had to do, and I still struggle with it. Maybe I always will. Time will tell. I understand that we can't continue to entertain the past if we expect to enjoy the present. Time is precious, and even if you weren't always at your best and doing your best, God did not give up on us. He saw what we could not see for ourselves, and he made his home in our heart when we allowed him to move in. It takes time to heal. I will agree, but move on and enjoy the blessings he has in store for you.

My prayer for today is that we all forgive ourselves and realize it was but for a season.

Amen and thank you, Lord.

Thought for the Day

Forgiveness frees you up to receive all the things in life that God intends to bless you with.

December 21

Prayer for the Day

Father, I wonder how many of us ponder the meaning of life. I know I do. Just when you think you have things figured out, along comes a bump in the road. The meaning of life changes with each passing day. I overthink everything, and I fret over things that tomorrow will hold no value, and who is to say there will be a tomorrow for one of us? The meaning of life is to be content as you go along, and do your best to rest on the promise the Lord gave us when he said he would never leave us nor forsake us. Each day has its own meaning and purpose.

My prayer for today is that we enjoy each day as it is given and rest comfortably in his precious arms.

Thought for the Day

Borrow a cup of sugar, not a cup of trouble.

December 22

Prayer for the Day

Father, I paid good money for a professional counselor to tell me I have a problem with boundaries. I love hard, and I want everyone to be happy.

Boundaries are put in place for our own protection and to ensure that we are treated well. You can still love and help people, but they must first learn to love themselves and want a good life for themselves. When you go too far, then all you have done is be an enabler. I have been very open and honest about my life in the hopes that I will help someone who struggles with the things I struggle with. I have a hard time saying no, but I'm learning that no is a real good answer sometimes, so now I'm working on being all right with saying no. Even the Lord knows he can't give his children a yes every time, and when he says no, we believe he still loves us. Am I right?

My prayer for today is that we learn to love ourselves first and help the ones we love understand that we loved them enough to know.

Amen and thank you, Lord.

Thought for the Day

Do you love me? Check yes or know.

December 23

Prayer for the Day

Father, it's very early, and I can hear the train from Lindale blowing its horn as it speeds down the tracks. For some years, I lived right beside those tracks, and I knew that train schedule as well as the conductor. I was not dependable back then. I couldn't even depend on myself, but I sure could depend on that train coming at certain times. A lot has changed since those lonesome days. It's a small town, so everyone knew I was walking in the dark literally, no power, water, and nothing else that a lot of people took for granted. I did not give up. I did not once think God was a myth or that he would not save me if only I asked. Looking back, I see that he had bigger and better things in store for me. When I pass that train track in Lindale, I always whisper, "Thank you, Jesus." I'm not an expert on anything, yet I freely tell about how he saved me with authority and confidence. I don't know what darkness you're facing, but we all do at times. I don't know if you believe you're too far gone to be saved. I can tell you this. He'll meet you where you stand, even at the railroad tracks.

My prayer for today is that we will live our lives with the knowledge that we are the one Jesus longs for, is looking for to spread his message of hope.

Yes, you are very special. Amen and thank you, Lord.

Thought for the Day

And the train rolls on.

December 24

Prayer for the Day

Father, it is the eve of your birth. I remember as a child how me and my brother and sister couldn't sleep for the excitement of waiting to rip into those presents we'd had our eyes on for days and days. Mama wrapped our presents so beautifully that it seemed like a terrible waste to even open up the present. She spent time on each one, adding just the right touch to each package to make it so unique. At family gatherings, you always knew what present Mama brought because it stood out and was different. It was unique. Just like those presents that were beautifully wrapped and unique, you are as well. You're not average, but you're specially wrapped because you were wrapped by Jesus himself, and he presented you to the world for his purpose and glory. The next time you look in the mirror, remember how beautifully you are wrapped, but also don't be afraid to tear it open to get to the good stuff.

My prayer for today is that we will consider ourselves as gifts from God and as a gift present ourselves to the world as unique.

Amen and thank you, Lord.

Thought for the Day

The past is gone. The future is unknown.
Today you are the present.

December 25

Prayer for the Day

Father, and so it is Christmas. Is it a merry Christmas? Not for us this year. Something and the absence of so many loved ones made it different and sad and just didn't have the feeling I was used to having around the holiday season. When I told my husband, "Merry Christmas," this morning, he asked me if Santa Clause left us anything, and I told him, "Yes, each other."

I would love to be somewhere watching the expressions on the faces of little kids tearing into presents so excited. Yes, we know the true meaning of Christmas and that unto us a Savior was born, and we thank God for this, but there is something so magical about that early morning feeling of Christmas and children.

My prayer for today is that your good memories never fade and that we can always remember that special time gone by and be happy to know we once were happy.

Amen and thank you, Lord.

Thought for the Day

I do know the difference between happiness and joy. Happiness is fleeting, and joy lasts forever.

December 26

Prayer for the Day

Father, it's the day after the day of Jesus's birth. Things will begin to get back on schedule and return to normal. I like schedules because they make me aware of what I'm doing for the day. Like my neighbors have a schedule of when they come down the drive way for work, I'm sitting in my happy place on schedule, and down they come on schedule. The time may vary a little to allow for the weekend, but for the most part, they are on schedule. Most things can be scheduled. Some things cannot be scheduled. Sometimes things are just not something you are able to plan for. Are we able to handle life when it's not on schedule?

My prayer for today is that we will allow the leading of the Holy Spirit to work in us when life does not go as planned. Even if we did not know what was going to happen, he did.

Amen and thank you, Lord.

Thought for the Day

They say fences make good neighbors.
I say good neighbors are just good neighbors.
I am blessed with good neighbors.

December 27

Prayer for the Day

Father, I have good friends. I mean the kind of friends that will be there for me any time of the day or night. What a blessing.

As we grow older, we have a smaller circle that we travel in; we see fewer people for various reasons. Life is so different as we get older. We begin to think about things we never thought about when we were young. The aches and pains are something we learn to adjust to, and we just do the best we can. Some of us realize how blessed we are to be embracing being older because if not for the grace of God, we wouldn't even be here. A slower pace brings more peaceful results; it is what I have found.

My prayer for today is that we will take time to enjoy each day and treat each day as one that was given and not promised. If we're still here, we still have purpose.

Amen and thank you, Lord.

Thought for the Day

Find your pain, and you'll find your purpose.

December 28

Prayer for the Day

Father, I have a phone that hardly ever rings. Oh, it used to ring when I was not practicing this thing called *tough love*. First of all, do the words *tough* and *love* even go together? Do they make sense together? I don't know, but I know it'll stop your phone from ringing. Sort of like my friends and some of my family are wondering why I paid a counselor good money to tell me I needed to set up boundaries when they weren't charging me a dime for the same excellent advice. I agree. It is hard to say no to someone you have always said yes to, and the yes answer is all they know. It's harder on me than it is for them because I'm miserable and worrying myself about it, but I'm getting stronger just as I pray they are.

My prayer for today is that we will be stronger than we feel and know that doing the right thing sometimes hurts but that God himself will hold us up because he never, not even once, let us down.

Amen and thank you, Lord.

Thought for the Day

If we don't love ourselves first, we cannot love anyone else.

December 29

Prayer for the Day

Father, I love rocking chairs. When I'm in my rocking chair, I can be still yet be moving at the same time. I get a lot of things settled in my rocking chair. I can't solve the world's problems when I rock, but for a little while, I can settle mine. It's comforting. Babies love to be rocked. It's soothing for them just as it's soothing for me. I've put a lot of miles on my rocking chair yet gone nowhere.

Sometimes going nowhere and doing nothing is exactly perfect. This world is a busy place, and we face a battle of some sort everywhere we turn. Take some time for yourself.

My prayer for today is that we will learn to accept our quiet time as a necessary tool to refresh what may be tired in us using whatever means necessary to gain strength.

Amen and thank you, Lord.

Thought for the Day

Whatever you do, rock it!

December 30

Prayer for the Day

Father, I see hotels and eateries that have a sign that says, "Pet friendly." We're pet friendly at my house, and I know plenty of people whose homes are pet friendly. What if we hung a sign around our neck saying, "People friendly," identifying ourselves as people lovers since everyone is not? Having a bad day? Are you still people friendly? Not feeling well? Still friendly to people? Sadly, our mood and circumstances dictate how friendly we are.

My prayer for today is that we will always follow the golden rule and love people even if we don't feel so friendly. Father, instill in us the love of Jesus all day, every day.

Amen and thank you, Lord.

Thought for the Day

Being kind costs nothing yet brings unexpected joy.

December 31

Prayer for the Day

Father, I'm impatient. Every morning, I get up and build a fire, and I want it to blaze and throw flames instantly, so when it only has embers, I start blowing on the embers until I nearly pass out. It'll catch fire and throw flames again because I have prepared my fire with wood, but if I don't see flames, I think nothing is happening. So I'm impatient and wrong. It dawned on me that I treat my relationship with the Lord the same way. I want immediate action, right-now results. His ways are not our ways, and his thoughts are so much higher than our thoughts, and if that wasn't enough, he is always right on time.

My prayer for today is that instead of trying to rush what I want to happen, I will wait for the Lord to decide the timing of what is to happen. We must rest on his word. He's never yet broken a promise.

Amen and thank you, Lord.

Thought for the Day

Yes, fire is used for warmth, but it is also used to refine.

About the Author

Meredith is a true inspiration. She has faced many challenges and heartbreak in life. She has been knocked down many times, but her faith is strong.

Meredith has touched so many lives with her compassion and encouragement. She embodies the term *prayer warrior*.

Meredith is a humble servant, always offering a smile, hug, and most importantly, a prayer.

CPSIA information can be obtained
at www.ICGtesting.com
Printed in the USA
FSHW010210131219
64791FS